AF019

MASSIMILIANO AFIERO

AXIS FORCES 19

WW2 AXIS FORCES

The Axis Forces 019 - First edition October 2021by Luca Cristini Editor for the brand Soldiershop
Cover & Art Design by soldiershop factory. ISBN code: 978-88-93277969

The Axis Forces number 19 – October 2021

Direction and editing: Via San Giorgio, 11 – 80021 AFRAGOLA (NA) -ITALY

Managing and Chief Editor: Massimiliano Afiero

Email: maxafiero@libero.it - **Website**: www.maxafiero.it

Contributors

Tomasz Borowski, Grégory Bouysse, Stefano Canavassi, Carlos Caballero Jurado, Rene Chavez, Gary Costello, Paolo Crippa, Carlo Cucut, Antonio Guerra, John B. Köser, Lars Larsen, Christophe Leguérandais, Eduardo M. Gil Martínez, Michael D. Miller, Peter Mooney, Péter Mujzer, Ken Niewiarowicz, Erik Norling, Raphael Riccio, Marc Rikmenspoel, Samcevich Andrei, Hugh Page Taylor, Charles Trang, Cesare Veronesi, Sergio Volpe

Editorial

Finally, here is the latest issue of our magazine, coming amidst a thousand logistical and organizational difficulties, which we always hope to put behind us every time but which seem to continue to plague us despite our best efforts. The important thing is that you continue as our readers and make our publication known as much as possible to your friends who may be interested in the military history of the Second World War. In the near future we are planning numerous new articles on topics less known and less covered by official historiography, naturally focusing our attention on Axis military formations. There will be more space devoted to battles and campaigns, including the war in the Pacific, and more space for the Navy and Air Force units of the various Axis countries. Of course, we always look forward to your requests and preferences on any topics you would like to see more of in the magazine. Feel free to write us or send us your emails. Let's now analyze the contents of this new issue of the magazine. We begin with the deployment of the Polizei Division on the Eastern Front, in the early summer of 1941. For the biographies, this time we address one of the best known and most famous officers of the Waffen-SS, *Gerd Bremer, who served first in the* Leibstandarte *Division and then in the* Hitlerjugend. *We continue with the third part of our study on* Frikorps Danmark, *as always accompanied by numerous and interesting photographs. The second part of the article dedicated to Walloon volunteers on the Eastern Front follows and we close with the story of Quisling's personal guard. Happy reading everyone and see you in the next issue.*

Massimiliano Afiero

The publication of The Axis Forces deals exclusively with subjects of a historical military nature and is not intended to promote any type of political ideology either present or past, as it also does not seek to exalt any type of political regime of the past century or any form of racism.

Contents

The Polizei-Division on the Eastern Front

By Massimiliano Afiero

A *Polizei-Division* column on the march, Summer 1941.

The attack to the north

While the train convoys were carrying the men of the *Polizei-Division* to the east, Dünaburg (Daugavpils, in Latvia) had already been taken by German troops. On June 22, 1941, the forces of *Heeresgruppe Nord* under *Generalfeldmarschall* Ritter von Leeb had attacked between Memel and Suwalki with *18.Armee* (Küchler) to the north and with *16.Armee* (Busch) to the south. The two armies flanked Hoepner's *Panzergruppe 4* which was attacking in the center. The armored group consisted of Manstein's *LVI.Armee-Korps* which in turn consisted of *8.Panzer-Division*, *3.Infanterie-Division* and *290.Infanterie-Division*. Manstein attacked towards Dünaburg with *8.Pz.Div.*, followed by troops of *3.Infanterie-Division*. After having seized Dünaburg, with the bulk of

Polizei artillery regiment troops on the march.

Polizei **infantrymen on the march, Summer 1941.**

Soldiers of the *Polizei-Division*, Summer 1941.

the German forces still about a hundred kilometers to the rear, Manstein had to wait several days before he could resume his advance. It was not until June 29 that all of the units of the corps finally reached the city. During the early phase of the campaign on the Eastern front, the *Polizei* division was kept in Army Group North reserve, ready to be committed wherever the situation warranted. On June 28, the first *Polizei* units to cross the Soviet border were the *I./Polizei-Artillerie-Regiment* and *Polizei-Schützen-Regiment* 2. After having marched in enemy territory in stifling heat and with their heavy weapons towed mainly by horses, the men of the division halted for the night at Sikiai, in Lithuania. At the same time, after the Soviets had suffered heavy losses and pulled pack along the entire front, they were attempting to organize strong resistance along the main line of resistance south of Lake Peipus, the so-called Stalin Line, which wound its way along the old Soviet border. The Soviet high command was particularly concerned with protecting the main communications nodes of Pleskau, Ostrov and Opotschka, using its armored formations. For their part, the German armored forces reached the Opotschka area on July 4, before Soviet reinforcements were able to arrive, allowing *Panzergruppe Hoepner* to resume the attack and cross the Düna (Dvina) River. The next objective of *Panzergruppe 4* was to advance along the Pleskau-Luga road towards Leningrad, while *LVI.Armee-Korps* was to cut the Opotschka - Ostrov road situated further to the east and reach Tschudovo, blocking the Moscow-Leningrad highway. On July 6, the *Totenkopf-Division* was able to break through the Stalin Line at Sebesch, opening the way for other German forces.

The advance of German units continued towards Opotschka, which was taken on July 7. Meanwhile, *18.Armee* had advanced further north, passing through Libau and Riga along the Baltic coast, across Latvia and Estonia. On 10 July, the advance units of *XXXXI.Armee-Korps* reached Pleskau and the southern shore of Lake Peipus, cutting off the Soviet divisions in the Baltics. In 18 days, *Heeresgruppe Nord* had covered two-thirds the distance that separated it from Leningrad. During the fighting, some twenty enemy divisions had been decimated, scattered, and in art completely annihilated. The conquest of Leningrad now seemed close at hand.

The Polizei-Division in action

On July 11, 1941, units of the *Polizei-Division* finally reached the Düna. The first to reach the banks of the river were elements of the *Polizei-Artillerie-Regiment*, which were completely horse-drawn. On July 13, *I./Pol.Art.Rgt.* crossed the river at Dryssa, using a bridge built by German engineers. Mülverstedt personally directed the river crossing by his men. On July 14, *I* and *III* groups of the *Polizei* artillery were ordered to provide support to *253.Infanterie Division*. The infantry division's advance encountered no resistance, because Soviet units had already withdrawn; the *Polizei* gunners therefore limited themselves to firing a few harassing rounds against enemy positions.

***Generalleutnant* Mülverstedt supervising the building of a brigde over the Düna (C.F.).**

On July 17, as the advance resumed, the *Polizei* was transferred from *L.Armee-Korps* and subordinated directly to *16.Armee*. The division's units advanced along the Dubrovo-Kuluschino-Grorowatka road, all the while under an oppressive heat. In addition, the route had been heavily mined by Soviet soldiers who fought throughout their retreat. Major Frosch's engineers had to work hard to open lanes throughout the sector and to clear the ground. The *Polizei* units were in the same operational sector as *Totenkopf* and were used mainly to carry out sweeps to try to intercept and wipe out isolated enemy units. On July 23, the division was operationally subordinated to *18.Armee*. On July 25, *Polizei* units were in the area east of Lake Peipus, continuing to advance towards

Leningrad. The next day they reached Pleskau, where they were visited by the chief of the *Ordnungspolizei*, General Kurt Daluege.

Polizei-Division **horsemen crossing the Düna River (*Carlo Fattoretto collection*).**

Major **Frosch on the Düna River.**

Memoirs of *Leutnant* Habeck of *III.Polizei-Schüzen-Regiment 3* regarding unit movements: '...*The regiment was on the march for several days. With a suffocating heat, on dusty roads, with rain that made marching impossible, our advance had turned into a Calvary. Even our four-footed friends* (the horses) *suffered as we did, especially those which carried heavy loads*'.

After a nighttime march, the artillery units reached Ostrov, bivouacking north of the city. On July 27, the division, subordinate to *Panzergruppe 4*, was ordered to take part in the attack against Luga, one of the main fortresses built by the Soviets along the road to Leningrad. The next day the division was resubordinated to von Manstein's *LVI.ArmeeKorps*. On the afternoon of July 30, the units began to move to the north. The artillery regiment's IV Group moved from Sapolje towards Wolosskowitschi. The regiment's *I Group* marched during the night under heavy Soviet artillery shelling. It was the first real contact with the Soviets. On the morning of July 31, the Soviets again hit the *Polizei* positions with heavy fire. In the afternoon the division's infantry units were engaged in supporting *8.Pz.Div.* tanks, with *Pol.-Schtz.-Rgt.1* on the right flank and *Pol.-Schtz.-Rgt.3* on the left flank. In particular, the infantrymen of *Pol.-Schtz.-Rgt.1* were engaged in the Staraja Szeriedka rea. At that time, the main combat line ran from the Domkino hills to Lake Wrewo.

A *Polizei* artillery regiment column moving to the north, Summer 1941.

***Polizei* horse-mounted scouts.**

To the right of the *Polizei* positions were units of *3.Infanterie-Division*, while on the left were troops of *269.Infanterie-Division*. The positions held by the *269.Inf.Div.* infantry had been heavily attacked by the Soviets with massive support of armored forces. The German units had nevertheless managed to rebuff all of the attacks and had held their positions. Meanwhile, the *Polizei* reconnaissance battalion had been sent to the Ljublino sector to secure the Gorodetz-Sapljuske road, not far from the southern shore of Lake Wrewo and at the same time was to reconnoiter the area to the south. Many prisoners were taken during these recon missions. On August 3, along the Sapljuske road, the *Polizei* recon troops were involved in bitter clashes against Soviet units, resulting in one soldier killed and three wounded.

***Polizei* soldiers taking a break during the march.**

The reconnaissance battalion continued to be engaged in combat in the lake area independently until August 10.

Further advance forward

With the deployment of the units along the new front line, the *Polizei* awaited new movement orders. No one yet knew that the next strategic objective was Luga, only ten kilometers from the positions they had just occupied. Not far from the sector held by *Polizei-Schützen-Regiment 3* right on the division's next axis of attack, was a stream that flowed from west to east and on whose banks was a large mill. The recon patrols had not been able to determine where the enemy defenses were located. Along the opposing lines of the front the first objective was the village of Kut, which was thought to have been abandoned by the enemy. Where the stream with the mill crossed the railway line, to the west of Kut, was the village of Smerdi. The *Polizei* unit commanders didn't have any other information. On August 1, the first to move forward were the infantrymen of *Polizei-Schützen-Regiment 3*, who without being seen by the enemy were able to establish good positions for the artillery forward observers.

Horse-drawn *Polizei* units marching northward (*Carlo Fattoretto collection*).

Shortly after, several forward batteries began to shell the enemy's advanced positions. *II./Pol.Schtz.Rgt.3,* led by *Hauptmann* Konopacki, advanced towards Kut. After recon patrols reported that the village had been abandoned by the Soviets, a platoon from 5.*Kompanie* moved towards the western edge of the position.

***Polizei* recon elements on the march, Summer 1941 (*Michael Cremin Collection*).**

***Polizei-Division* infantry marching toward Luga (MC).**

The Soviets withdrew to the north of the Kut-Smerdi road before *III./Pol.Schtz.Rgt.3* under *Hauptmann* Rehfeldt arrived on scene. On August 2, several patrols on the left sector ran into strong enemy concentrations, discovering a Soviet artillery battery hidden behind the mill. The *Pol.Schtz.Rgt.3* commander, *Oberst* Wünnenberg, decided to schedule an attack in force the next day on both sides of the mill, using an infantry company in the right-hand sector and another three on the left. After having advanced for a few hundred meters, the *Polizei* infantry were quickly stalled by massive fire from the Soviets, who had dug in well and had many heavy weapons. Soon after, *6./Pol.Schtz.Rgt.3* was ordered to advance to the north of Kut. Following is the testimony of *Obergefreiter* Schel of that unit: '*...It was our first attack. We found ourselves facing a thick forest from which they were shooting at us. After we got in amongst the trees and had gotten through the forest, we found that*

The area southwest of Leningrad involved in the fighting.

***Polizei* infantry attacking over open ground (*Cremin*).**

***Polizei* infantry attacking with tank support (*Cremin*).**

the Soviets had set up a strong line of bunkers'. Taken by surprise by the strong enemy resistance, the *Polizei* infantrymen were forced to seek shelter in the forest, where they reorganized and administered aid to the many wounded. Among the wounded was the *III./3* commander, *Hauptmann* Rehfeldt. The only effect these attacks had was to determine Soviet behavior and reaction in that sector.

The attack against Luga

The offensive against Luga, scheduled for 7 August, had to be postponed because of heavy rains. On the afternoon of 9 August, the code word *'Berlin'*, to begin the attack, was given to the units. Von Manstein had planned to conquer the city with a movement from the south; the *Polizei-Division* was to seize enemy positions north of Smerdi. However, the units did not begin to move until 10 August. The orders for *LVI.Armee-Korps* were to attack the enemy positions on both sides of Luga, with the *schwerpunkt* (the point of major effort) to the west of the city.

Testimony of *Hauptmann* Radtke, adjutant of *Polizei-Schützen-Regiment 2*, regarding these encounters: '*...Following preparatory artillery fire, the division launched its first major attack in Russia as part of* LVI.Armee-Korps. *With two regiments on the line, the attack was led personally by the division*

Polizei-Division **infantrymen moving to attack enemy position south of Luga, Summer 1941.**

commander General *Mülverstedt. The division was able to take the enemy positions north of Smerdi, breaking deep into the enemy defensive line. Offensive and defensive combat lasted throughout the day against seasoned enemy units. The enemy repeatedly committed armored forces. With the favorable wooded terrain and thanks to many defensive works, the Soviets were able to halt our advance in the late evening. The division reported heavy losses. Enemy losses were even heavier…In the following days, the division's mission was to make limited local attacks against enemy positions. At the same time, the German headquarters ordered the division to move to Udraika front, east of the road that led to Leningrad. The* Polizei-Division *was initially to attack and destroy enemy positions along the river. Soon after it was to turn to the north and seize the city of Luga by an attack from the east of the Luga River. By continuing to engage the enemy with an attack in the sector to the west of the road and shifting the* schwerpunkt *to the sector to the east of the road, the Soviets could be taken by surprise. In addition, the division was able to achieve modest success by its artillery fire, with a diversionary attack along the Udraika River. The attack on the division's flank, particularly the attack by* Oberst *Schulze and his* Polizei-Schützen-Regiment 2, *made it possible to seize all of the Udraika sector on the first day of the fighting. Our losses were relatively limited. Enemy losses, especially in prisoners, were instead very high. At dawn on the second day of the attack the regiment continued to advance. Enemy forces tried desperately to reorganize, but because of the strong pressure exerted by the division west of the road, the Soviets were able to do precious little. The men of* Polizei-Schützen-Regiment 2 *were able to overwhelm the last enemy defenses and conquer Luga.*

A *Polizei* NCO observing the course of the battle.

***Oberst* Schülze, right, discussing orders with his NCOs.**

This success opened the road for the German forces towards Leningrad. However, in the fighting the division lost its commandant, General *Mülverstedt.*

General Mülverstedt fell in combat while he was leading his men's attack against the enemy positions in the forest. In that first baptism of fire for the *Polizei* on the Eastern front, he wanted to personally lead operations on the battlefield. Accompanied by his aide, *Leutnant* Reimer, he wore a camouflage smock and was carrying a machine pistol. While he was urging his men, who were stalled by a massive amount of fire unleashed by the enemy, to go forward, a sudden torrent of mortar fire landed on top of them, forcing them to throw themselves to the ground. *Generalleutnant* Mülverstedt, who had knelt down to observe the terrain, got up and again urged his men to press the attack. It was just at that moment that a mortar fragment hit him full in the chest. An NCO and three men quickly carried him to the aid station at Iljishe Proroge, where the *2./Polizei-Sanitäts-Abteilung* under *Oberst Dr.* Ott was located. When the men got there, however, the doctor could only confirm the death of their commander. Command of the division was assumed a few days later by *SS-Brigadeführer* Walter Kruger, who until that time had been the chief of staff of the *Polizei.* That same day, *Oberleutnant* Hermann Hirschmüller, commanding *2./Pol.Schtz.Rgt.2* and *Hauptmann* Hubert Abele, commander of *4./Pol.Schtz.Rgt.2,* were also killed.

***Polizei* infantry on the march, 1941.**

***Polizei* soldiers in the Kut Forest, 1941.**

Soviet prisoners being sent to the rear, 1941.

The attack against Stojanowtschina

During the morning of August 11, *Hauptmann* Konopacki's *II./Pol.Schtz.Rgt.3* attacked to the west of the mill to try to ease enemy pressure against *I./Pol.Schtz.Rgt.3* led by Major Fricke. The *Polizei* infantrymen had to be careful when moving because the entire area had been heavily mined by the Soviets. After having managed to clear a gap, *I./3* was engaged in attacking the position at Stojanowtschina, while *II./3* was moving towards Lake Rakowitzkoje. At the same time, the regimental commander, *Oberst* Wünnenberg, ordered *III./3* to circle around the enemy positions on the left with some of its men, to hit the enemy defensive positions in front of the village from behind. The attack by *I./3* was successful and during the afternoon Fricke's infantrymen gained the heights north of Sojanowtschina. The Soviets reacted quickly, counterattacking with tanks supported by artillery fire; the first enemy armored attack was directed against *I./Pol.Schtz.Rgt.2.* Four enemy tanks were destroyed or captured during the fighting, but *Polizei* losses were also high. *Pol.Schtz.Rgt.2* tried to break into enemy defenses around the Stojanowtschina area, but with no success. It was not until the night between August 11 and 12 that the *I./3* infantry were able to take Stojanowtschina. The rifle companies were then ordered to dig in in place and to hold their new positions. During that same night, while attempting a counterattack, two Soviet tanks were knocked out by the regiment's 37mm antitank guns. At dawn on August 12, the Soviets attacked again with tanks, focusing particular effort against the *II./Pol.Schtz.Rgt.3* positions. Some enemy tanks were knocked out with hand grenades at close range. In a matter of a few minutes, another twelve enemy tanks were destroyed by antitank fire, while another was destroyed with hand grenades. Around 10:00, *1./Pol.Schtz.Rgt.3* forward observers communicated via radio: '...*Enemy tanks approaching our position*'. This time there were three tanks weighing 52 tons, against which the 37mm antitank guns could do little.

A *Polizei* soldier directing a soviet prisoner to the rear area, Summer 1941.

A German soldier armed with an MP38, Summer 1941.

Two other smaller tanks were knocked out, while the others withdrew. Around 13:00, the Soviets attacked again, intensifying pressure along the entire sector. In the afternoon, the appearance of *Stuka* dive bombers stabilized the situation and removed any further threats. Enemy artillery, almost for spite, began to hit the *Polizei* positions with heavy fire for hours, causing fresh losses. Among the dead was *Hauptmann* Kruse, commander of

3./Polizei-Pionier-Bataillon. Testimony of gunner Herbert Rauchwetter of *II./Pol.Schtz.Rgt.3*: *'...During the night between 11 and 12 August, we were ordered to assume positions at Stojanowtschina. Stoja, as we called it. I emplaced my antitank gun on a small rise and finished preparing my position around midnight. It was time to sleep! I settled down near the gun's trail and fell asleep almost right away. Around 3:00 I was awakened by sharp noises, a sign that enemy tanks were approaching our position. Because of the fog, I couldn't see much.*

A Soviet tank has just been spotted by a *Polizei-Division* 37 mm *Pak* and hastily emplaced, with several infantrymen, on the right, take cover behind some trees (*Michael Cremin Collection*).

A Soviet tank in flames, Summer 1941.

I wasn't able to see the first enemy tank clearly until it was only three meters away. I quickly fired a first round, then a second. A sudden flame and the tank was enveloped in fire, lighting up the scene in front of my position. We barely made it in time to duck to avoid the many fragments that flew around us. I saw another six tanks approaching us, but the mist still prevented me from getting a good sight picture on them. When we finally managed to target one, I fired. The flames that rose from the knocked-out hulk allowed me to spot the other enemy tanks. With a series of accurate shots, I was able to hit them one after another, in rapid sequence. To knock out seven tanks, I used nine hollow charge rounds and four high explosive. The next day the regimental commander, Oberst *Wünnenberg, paid us a visit and congratulated us, shaking everyone's hands. He promoted my gun chief to* Feldwebel. *On September 19, 1941, I was awarded the Iron Cross First Class'.*

***Polizei* soldiers posing for a photo next to a destroyed KV-2 tank (*Carlo Fattoretto Collection*).**

Readying a *Stielhandgranate*.

On August 12, contact was re-established with *269.Infanterie-Division,* thanks to several patrols sent out by the *Polizei* towards the positions held by their army comrades. In particular, patrols led by *Unterfeldwebel* Gramatke and by *Unteroffizier* Wieland were able to advance towards the railway embankment and after several clashes with enemy infantry, managed to make contact with the army elements.

The situation on the Luga front

On August 15, 1941, *von Manstein's LVI.Armee-Korps* was relieved by Lindemann's *L.Armee-Korps and the Polizei* became subordinate to it. At the same time, General Reinhardt's *XXXXI.Armee-Korps* reached the Kingisepp (Jamburg)-Wolossowo railway line after having been in tough fighting and taken heavy losses. Its units had gotten to within sixty kilometers of Leningrad and only thirty kilometers from

Gatschina. In order to continue the offensive against Leningrad, it was however necessary to eliminate the enemy forces at Luga as soon as possible, employing mainly the *Polizei* and *269.Infanterie-Division*, subordinated to *L.Armee-Korps*.

***Polizei* soldiers in the forests south of Luga (*Charles Trang Collection*).**

***Polizei* soldiers sheltering before a new attack (*Cremin*).**

On the morning of August 16, General von Manstein was on the road to Dno, going to Generaloberst Busch's *16.Armee* headquarters. At the same time, *3.Infanterie-Division* moved eastwards in the *L.Armee-Korps* rear area and the *Totenkopf-Division* was withdrawn from the front line. These two divisions were to attack the flank and rear area of the Soviet 34th Army. While the *X.Armee-Korps* divisions, located south of Lake Ilmen, were seriously threatened by Soviet attacks, on that same day of August 16, the troops of *I.Armee-Korps* seized

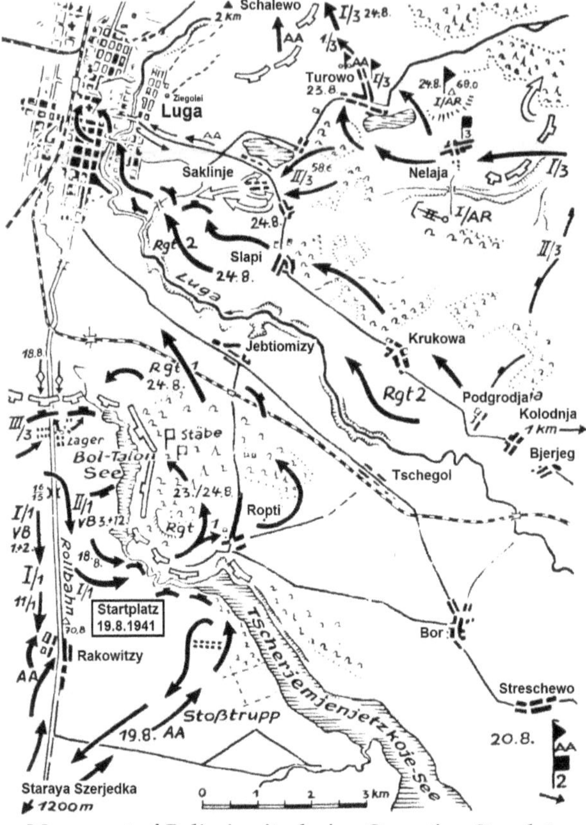

Movement of *Polizei* units during Operation *Starplatz*.

***Polizei* soldiers in the forest south of Luga (*Cremin*).**

Novgorod, fifty kilometers further to the north and General Lindemann went to *Polizei* headquarters to impart new orders: his new plan called for closing the Soviet forces in a pocket between the two lakes south of Luga (*Unternehmen Starplatz*, Operation 'Departure Point'). In that area the Soviets had concentrated many forces, well entrenched in the forests. *Polizei-Schützen-Regiment 3* was ordered to make a frontal attack against the enemy in order to force him to withdraw. For the action it was to be reinforced by several engineer platoons and by *1./Pol.Pz.Jg.Abt.* In particular, *II./Pol.Schtz.Rgt.3* was to capture a group of houses that occupied both sides of the road.

The attack began well, with *I.* and *II.Bataillon* advancing and encountering hardly any resistance, although the infantrymen of *III./3* ran into a minefield and were forced to stop. The assault groups of *I./Pol.Schtz.Rgt.1* and *II.Pol.Schtz.Rgt.1* faced a similar situation. In spite of everything, a recon patrol led by *Leutnant* Luger was able to get as far as the group of houses, reporting that they could be easily taken. Three rifle companies of *III./Pol.Schtz.Rgt.3* were thrown into the attack, ably led by *Hauptmann* Reinke. Following furious hand-to-hand fighting, the enemy was forced to fall back. The next day the fighting shifted to the village of Ropti, where a *Pol.Schtz.Rgt.1* attack group was committed. At the same time, *Stossgruppe Miersch* (led by *Major* Miersch, the *I./Pol.Schtz.Rgt.1* commander) made contact with the *Polizei-Aufkl.-Abteilung* at Staraja

A *Polizei* infantryman attacking, Summer 1941.

A *Polizei* 37 mm *Pak* in firing position.

Szerjedka. Until that moment the *Polizei* recon battalion had been engaged in the isthmus between the two lakes. The ring around the enemy forces had tightened gradually and all attempts to break out were eliminated. After having left the positions that had just been conquered to troops of *269.Infanterie-Division*, the *Polizei* was committed to continuing the advance towards Luga, attacking from the east, along the banks of the river. On August 22, *III./Pol.Schtz.Rgt.3* was disbanded and its remaining personnel were distributed to the regiment's two other battalions.

The conquest of Luga

On August 23, *Polizei-Division* troops attacked enemy forces at Syretz and in the Udrajka sector. After destroying them, they continued their advance towards Luga and seized it. *I./Polizei-Schützen-Regiment 3* had its first contact with the enemy southeast of Syretz. Enemy resistance was quickly overcome and the battalion reported the capture of the city that same day. The battalion's advance then continued towards Kolodja, while troops of *II./3* occupied the heights to the west of Wybor. While the rifle battalions continued their advance, General Lindemann met with the commander of the *Polizei*, *SS-Brigdf.* Krüger, to discuss the next attack moves: the second objective of the offensive, between the two lakes, was reached without any fighting, *I./3* continued to advance, but having gotten to within a kilometer east of Nelaja, was checked by strong enemy resistance. In order to overcome it, additional antitank guns had to be brought in as reinforcements. *1.Kompanie*, leading the attack, reached Turovo and the hills northwest of there during the night. There, the battalion was heavily engaged against other enemy forces who were well hidden in the woods in front of the hills. These were finally neutralized and at least two hundred prisoners were taken. The next day, at 8:30, *Polizei* troops resumed the attack along the Turovo-Saklinje axis.

SS-Brigdf. **Walter Krüger (*Carlo Fattoretto*).**

A 37 mm *Pak* in action.

After having crossed the river, the remaining pockets of enemy resistance were wiped out. The Soviets launched a counterattack against the left flank, which was quickly repulsed. The *I./3* and a platoon from *14.Kompanie* seized the position at Schalewo, thus reaching the Luga-Leningrad road. Around noon, *Oberst* Schulze, commander of *Pol.Schtz.Rgt.2,* reported the capture of Luga to division headquarters. Enthusiasm for the capture of the city was reflected in a radio message that Schulze sent to division headquarters: '...*We are in the heart of Luga. Where is everybody else?...*'.What had happened? *Pol.Schtz.Rgt.2* had in fact opened a gap passing through Krukowa and Slapi, unhinging the Soviet defensive ring.

The work of the engineers, called upon to open passages through the numerous minefields and to neutralize other defensive traps prepared by the Soviets, contributed significantly to the capture of the city. Meanwhile, *Pol.Schtz.Rgt.3* continued to fight at Saklinje, Turovo and Schalewo supported by the reconnaissance battalion. *Pol.Schtz.Rgt.1* had managed to overcome enemy resistance between lakes Bol.Talon and Tcherjemien-Jetzkoje and to capture Ropti, killing at least three thousand Soviet soldiers in the clashes. Thanks to this major success, the road to Leningrad was open and the reputation of the *Polizei-Division* increased notably in the higher commands of the German army. Between August 10 and 24, 1941, *L.Armee-Korps* had destroyed 53 Soviet tanks, 28 artillery pieces, 13 antitank guns and had captured 1,937 prisoners.

The march northwards continues

On the morning of August 25, the *Polizei-Aufklärungs-Abteilung,* led by Major Wegener, was ordered to advance to the north towards Krupeli, along the road that led to Leningrad. The 1st Company was on the left and the 2nd on the right. The *Pak* platoon marched on the road itself while the 3rd Company's cannon platoon moved behind the 2nd Company. Around 18:00, a platoon from the 2nd Recon Company, along with an engineer platoon, was ordered to cross the Luga River at Ilsia and establish a bridgehead. Enemy artillery tried to hinder the movement of the *Polizei* units, without any success.

***Polizei-Aufklärungs-Abteilung* vehicles in the Staraya Szerjedka area (*Michael Cremin*).**

***Polizei* troops prepare to attack toward Luga.**

On August 26, the reconnaissance battalion was ordered to cross the Oredezh River. *122.Infanterie-Division* was to provide supporting fire from the north. Three Soviet infantry regiments counterattacked but were driven off by *Polizei* troops. After having crossed the Oredezh, the recon battalion continued on to the north; some of its recon patrols found that large enemy forces were present at Oserzy and along the banks of the Tschernaja. The *Polizei* recon troops were then ordered to secure the right flank of the advance of the *II./2*, but without heavy weapons the mission seemed impossible. On August 26, after only one day of rest, the *Polizei-Division* resumed its march northward, still subordinate to *L.Armee-Korps* along with *269.Infanterie-Division*. The troops passed through Mesowo and were involved in several clashes with the Soviet rear guard at Oredezh. On August 29, the division received a batch of new recruits who were parceled out to the artillery regiment, the infantry and the recon

Hauptmann Vockensohn, commander of *III./Pol.Sch.Rgt.2*, personally climbing the bell tower of the Luga cathedral to raise the Third Reich flag (Bottom Photo), watched by *Hauptmann* Helmut Dörner (Top Photo).

Polizei soldiers assaulting enemy positions, Summer 1941.

battalion. That same day orders arrived to reach Krassnogwardeisk and to destroy enemy forces before they could assemble at Leningrad. To the right of the *Polizei* was *96. Infanterie-Division*, subordinate to *XXVIII.Armee-Korps*. However, there were a few kilometers separating the two divisions and it was precisely in that gap that the Soviets attacked in an attempt to surround the German vanguard. Nevertheless, all of their attacks were repelled with a great expenditure of energy.

Amidst the Lugi marshes

The *Polizei* units continued their advance towards Lugi, a village located about six kilometers north of Lake Wjalje. Numerous enemy units, who were still putting up a fight, were spotted in the marshes around Lugi. The

Polizei-Aufklärungs-Abteilung was not far away, as it was still engaged on the Tschernaja River on both sides of Oserzi. On the morning of 29 August, *6./Pol.Schtz.Rgt.2* attacked and took Oserzi, thanks in part to support by divisional artillery. After the village had been taken, the recon battalion carried out reconnaissance further to the north; no contact was made with the enemy, because the Soviet units were falling back. A few kilometers from Pelkowo there was a brief firefight with an isolated Soviet unit that hastily withdrew. During the approach march, at Pelkowo, the *Polizei* troops encountered stronger Soviet resistance in the tough fighting that followed, and significant losses were sustained. The Soviets had set up a complex system of fortifications with many minefields behind the village. After having fended off the first German attack, the Soviets counterattacked, throwing sizeable forces into the fight. *II./Pol.Schtz.Rgt.2* reached the scene just as enemy pressure began to increase and quickly joined the attack at Pelkowo.

The capture of Luga was the first real success for the *Polizei-Division* on the Eastern Front. In the photo, *Hauptmann* Dörner and his men in a city park, next to a statue of Lenin (*Michael Cremin*).

A *Polizei* NCO wounded.

In the afternoon all of the Soviet positions were eliminated. At dawn on 30 August reconnaissance was carried out north of the village, after which strong enemy concentrations were spotted south of Lake Szerjeschno. Gathering its forces, *II./Pol.Schtz.Rgt.2* continued its advance northwards to the village of Ostrov, where there were renewed clashes with other enemy units. The troops of *III./2* were still busy with trying to capture Lugi.

Attacks against Krassnizy and Ssussanino

During the following days, *Polizei-Schützen-Regiment 1* was engaged in attacking the positions at SSussanino, supported by the batteries of *I./Polizei-Artillerie-Regiment*, while *269.Infanterie-Division* attacked towards Lukaschi. Oders for *Polizei-Schützen-Regiment 1* were: '*...To capture Ssussanino and, following its capture, to* *proceed along both sides of the road that leads from Sssussanino to Ssabory. The regiment must be ready to break through Soviet defensive positions covering its right flank south of the Lissino-Krassnogwardeisk railway line'.*

***Polizei* soldiers pose next to a *Horch* car. The *Polizei* caps have for the moment replaced their steel helmets. (*Charles Trang Collection*)**

Following fierce and bloody fighting, the village of Ssussanino was taken on 6 September. During the fighting the *Pol.Flak-Abt.* Commander, *Hauptmann* Greschuna, was killed. The previous day the recon battalion reached Paruschkino on the Luga-Leningrad road, then moved on towards Drushnaja Gorka, making contact with troops of *8.Panzer-Division* and *269.Infanterie-Division*. Also on 6 September, *Infanterie-Regiment 322* of the *285.Sicherungs-Division* was ordered to attack towards Ananewy and the *Polizei* recon troops were to cover the regiment's western flank the Soviets, however, had anticipated the German attack and attacked first. The *Polizei* recon battalion then made a ferocious counterattack, thus staving off the threat of a new enemy penetration. During the fighting, the battalion's 2nd Company suffered many killed and wounded.

That afternoon, *Inf.Rgt.322* was finally able to launch an attack, but in vain, as it was stalled by strong enemy resistance. It was not until the next morning, thanks to the support of several armored vehicles, that Ananewy was torn from the Soviet troops. During this same period, elements of *18.Armee*, *Panzergruppe 4* and the left flank of *16.Armee*, kicked off the offensive against Leningrad.

Bibliography

Massimiliano Afiero, "*4.SS-Polizei-Panzergrenadier-Division*", Associazione Culturale Ritterkreuz
Massimiliano Afiero, "The *4th Waffen-SS Panzergrenadier Division Polizei*", Schiffer Publishing

Gert Bremer

by Peter Mooney

SS-Obersturmführer **Gerhard Bremer.**

Leibstandarte **motorcyclists with some prisoners, 1941.**

Date of birth: 25.07.1917
SS Number: 310 405

His service began in April 1933 when he joined the *Hitler Youth,* staying there until April 1936. He then served in the *R.A.D.* from April 1936 until the start of October 1936. He followed this by entering the *SS* on the 6th of October 1936, initially serving in the III Battalion, SS-Regiment *Germania.* At the start of October 1937 he went to Bad Tolz, staying there until the 1st of September 1938. His next move came on the 9th of November the same year when he moved to the *LAH,* the same day as he was promoted to *SS-Untersturmfuhrer.* He went with the *LAH* into Poland during 1939 winning the Second Class Iron Cross on the 1st of October 1939. He then took part in the campaign in the west during the summer of 1940, winning the First Class Iron Cross on the 5th of June 1940. At the start of September 1940 he was promoted to *SS-Obersturmfuhrer.* Just over one month later, he received the Infantry Assault Badge in Bronze. Just prior to the start of *Barbarossa,* on the 21st of June 1941, he was promoted further to *SS-Hauptsturmfuhrer.* Bremer and the *LAH* then went east into Russia as part of Operation *Barbarossa.* Bremer and the rest of the *Aufklärungs Abteilung* took Dnjeprowka at the very end of September. The following day they moved towards Mentschekur, Bremer's

Leibstandarte motorcyclists on the Eastern Front.

Leibstandarte soldiers during an attack, Summer 1941.

Vehicles of the reconnaissance group of the *Leibstandarte* on the march, September 1941.

1. Kompanie were in Hf. Neuhof during this day. The next day he led his men in an attack against difficult opposition and took Jelissawetowka. By the end of the 3rd of October they had played their part in the defeat of two Russian Armies, fighting on the enemy's southern flank. Over ten thousand prisoners passed into captivity along with hundreds of guns. From there, the pursuit turned south and south east. The enemy had realized that they could not stop the advance of the Germans and those soldiers not already captured began a rapid flight eastwards. The importance of capturing objectives further to the east was essential for the *LAH* and their Kameraden. What developed was an intensive, fast paced race between the Russians and the *LAH,* led by Bremer's *1. Kompanie, Aufklärungs Abteilung.* The first objective reached in the 5th of October was Fedrowka, where Bremer cleared the town of the enemy. Next on the list was an important bridge at Terpenje, over the Moltschnaja River (I recommend that you read through Kurt Meyer's, '*Grenadiers*' book to get a full idea of the intensity of this advance). Bremer and his men led the race towards the bridge and as they did so, they found themselves in amongst a mass of enemy soldiers and Russian civilians all vying for the same objective. Bremer's men began to shoot into the enemy ranks in order to cut a path through the throng. As they got close to the bridge, the Russians detonated their explosive charges on the bridge – it was full of their own soldiers at the time. This apparent disaster did not stop Gert Bremer. His men sought and found a suitable crossing further along the river. They raced across it and established a small bridgehead, all of this within one hour of reaching the bridge itself.

SS-Ostuf. **Bremer with Ritterkreuz.**

This bridgehead was extended and the advance continued to the south east.

Knights Cross

On the 6th of October 1941 Astrachanka and Arechowka were taken and also an area near Nowospasskoje. The enemy was attempting to resist and the last two objectives were taken in close combat by Gert Bremer and his men. By the end of this day Romanowka was reached and senior Russian staff officers were captured. On the following day, early morning advances brought the *LAH* to within ten miles of Berdjansk. At Stanitsa Nowospasskoj, Bremer's 1. Kompanie once again raced into dense enemy columns and successfully crossed the bridge. From here Berdjansk beckoned. As the advance continued, the *Aufklärungs Abteilung* were made aware of retreating Russians coming from the west. They diverted, engaged and captured the enemy column containing two thousand enemy soldiers, with about five hundred being captured. Enemy survivors were surprised to be met by Germans this far eastwards. Once again, Bremer was in the lead here. As this took place Army units from Battalion von Boddien moved into Berdjansk. The *LAH* were to move upon Mariupol next. This objective was reached before midday on the 8th of October. Bremer's 1. Kompanie had led the way and pushed through the outer defenses and straight through the sprawling city itself. This success surprised even the German High Command. Due to the size of the city, the advances slowed as the entire city had to be controlled. This lasted for the next few days with the help of accompanying infantry. In summary, Gert Bremer had led most of the way from Dnjeprowka, through Fedrowka and on towards Berdjansk, finally reaching and seizing Mariupol. He did not do this alone and was helped by his *LAH* Kameraden, as well as Kameraden from the

SS-Ostuf. **Bremer with Kurt Meyer, Spring 1942.**

Leibstandarte **motorcyclists on the march, 1941.**

Heer. He did however, show great courage and leadership abilities during this time, as well as extreme cool headedness and bravery. His advances had often overtaken the massed ranks of the retreating enemy, a situation that would have had an incalculable psychological advantage. With Mariupol's capture, the 'Battle for the Sea of Azov' was considered to be over. Estimations placed one hundred thousand prisoners, along with hundreds of tanks and guns as the size of the booty. Gert Bremer certainly played a critical role in this success at the head of his 1. Kompanie, Aufklarungs Abteilung, *LAH.* His Knights Cross recommendation is not on his file, therefore the author and the submission date are unknown, but it can be presumed that Sepp Dietrich would have written this? What is known is that it was approved on the 30th of October 1941. Considering that his actions finished on the 8th of October, this was a rapid approval, compared to his *Waffen-SS* Kameraden. This award made him the 19th *Waffen-SS* soldier and the 5th *LAH* soldier to receive this award. He was presented with his medal on the 5th of November by Sepp Dietrich, Kurt Meyer was also present. Despite the addition of that high-level award, Bremer remained in his kompanie command role through to April 1943. In that time he added the following awards; the Infantry Assault Badge (12th of March 1942), the Bulgarian Bravery Medal (25th of July 1942), the Romanian Bravery Medal (20th of August 1942), the Russian Front Medal (21st of September 1942) and the Close Combat Clasp in Silver (25th of November 1943).

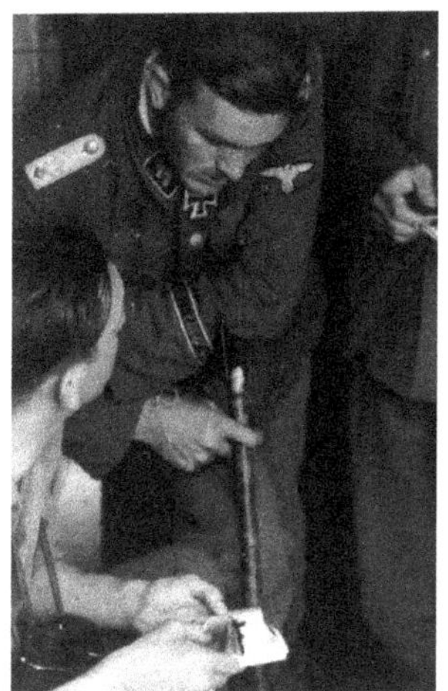

Other photos of the *SS-Ostuf.* Bremer with Kurt Meyer, Spring 1942.

***SS-Stubaf.* Bremer on the Western Front, 1944.**

Hitlerjugend Division

He was promoted to *SS-Hauptsturmfuhrer* back on the 21st of June 1942. He was one of a number of *LSSAH* soldiers that were selected to move to the new *Hitlerjugend Division* in the wake of the Kharkov campaign. Two months later, he was moved to the role of Battalion Commander within the above division. Helping to train the boys that filled the ranks of that renamed *12. SS-Panzer Division 'Hitlerjugend'*, he was promoted to *SS-Sturmbannfuhrer* on the 30th of January 1944. His command changed to that of the *Panzer Aufklärungs Abteilung* during April. It was that formation that he led during his next combat test, which was the Normandy fighting. His actions there earned him the addition of the German Cross in Gold, done on the 30th of August 1944. It was that same campaign that also resulted in him being submitted for the addition of the Oakleaves to his Knight's Cross. That document was compiled by his divisional commander, Kraemer, on the 4th of November 1944, and it detailed: '*During the first days of the Invasion the* SS-Pz.Aufkl.Abt. 12 *conducted a flank protection mission along the line Audrieu—Tilly sur Seulleswith great and far-reaching success. However the unit sustained heavy losses throughout both this operation and the subsequent fighting around Caen (in which it served as a ready reserve). The understrength* Abteilung *was thus dispatched to the area around Rugles (10 km northeast of Laigle) on the 28.7.1944 to partially refit.*

A signed photo of Bremer with Oakleaves.

While in this area the commander of the Abteilung, SS-Sturmbannführer *Bremer, received word from routing friendly troops about a thrust by strong enemy tank forces from the Laval area in the direction of Chartres. Upon hearing this he immediately dispatched all available forces to reconnoiter this enemy force. By doing this the higher commands learned of enemy transmissions that were sent in the clear. The hostile advance was consistently delayed by the reconnaissance patrols that remained in constant contact with the enemy.*

After friendly blocking formations had occupied the line Laigle—Verneuil the Abteilung *was ordered to move to the Evreux area by the Division on the 15.8.1944 so as to resume an accelerated refitting. As a result of independently dispatched reconnaissance at the line Dreux—Houdan—Mantes the Abteilung spotted a northward thrust by enemy armoured forces along both sides of the Eure river at a relatively early time. The available weak forces, together with the support of* Kampfgruppe Wahl, *subsequently occupied a blocking line at the Eure river. The tireless and skillfully employed reconnaissance brought about a clear understanding of the enemy situation and significantly delayed their forward advance. These measures were taken by* SS-Sturmbannführer *Bremer on his own initiative and in an unclear situation. They decisively contributed to the prevention of the enemy's intent to cut off major friendly forces while they were still withdrawing on the western side of the Seine. He and his weak forces tied down much larger enemy forces, delayed their advance and inflicted significant losses. He personally applied himself to the combat on a continual basis in a ruthless and exemplary fashion.*

I hold Bremer as worthy, on account of his unconditional readiness for duty and the bravery that he has repeatedly demonstrated while in difficult situations, of being awarded the Oakleaves to the Knight's Cross of the Iron Cross.'

Onto the same document, Sepp Dietrich (now commanded the *6. Panzerarmee*) added his endorsement. The submission was approved on the 26th of November 1944. He continued to lead the above formation until the end of the war, receiving a further promotion to *SS-Obersturmbannfuhrer* on the 20th of April 1945. He survived the war and died on the 29th of October 1989.

Bibliography

Peter Mooney, "*Waffen-SS Knights and their Battles*", Schiffer Publishing
A. Kwasny, G.Kwasny, "*Die Eichenlaubträger 1940-1945*", Deutsches Wehrkundearchiv
J.W. Schneider, "*Their Honor was Loyalty!*", R. James Bender Publishing
Tim Saunders, Richard Hone, "*12th Hitlerjugend SS Panzer Division in Normandy*", Pen & Sword

Danish volunteers on the Eastern front 1941-1943

by Massimiliano Afiero

SS-Stubaf. **Hans Albert von Lettow-Vorbeck.**

New battles

On June 10, 1942, the new commander of *Frikorps*, *SS-Stubaf.* Hans Albert von Lettow-Vorbeck(1) arrived, the grandson of the legendary commander of the German troops in Tanzania during the First World War. The appointment of a German officer was considered by the Danish volunteers as a new violation of the agreements established at the time of the creation of the Legion, so von Lettow-Vorbeck was greeted coldly upon his arrival. After all, *SS-Hstuf.* Martinsen had proven his competence as an officer in the field, but was virtually unknown at the High Command SS. The new commander came from the legendary *Wiking* division and was initially designated to command the Flemish SS Legion, then was diverted to the Danish formation. Despite the coldness shown by his new soldiers, von Lettow-Vorbeck proved to be very helpful, meeting the volunteers personally, asking questions about their families and their country. The discontent among the troops thus began to fade. Meanwhile, the Soviets were preparing to take back Bolshoje Dubovizy. During the night of June 10, 1942, the Soviets launched a full-scale attack on the German defensive line north of Bolshoje Dubovizy. At 22:00, an alarming message arrived at the command post of the *Frikorps*: "*... enemy counterattack in progress!*". After the first moment of panic, a quick retreat was ordered, after midnight, to

A Danish defensive position with an *MG-34.*

German assault guns on the Demyansk front, 1942.

Infantry soldiers attack Soviet positions.

safer positions about two kilometers north of Vassiljevschtschina while the position of Bol.Dubovizy was abandoned. At the same time, *SS-Stubaf.* von Lettow-Vorbeck began organizing the first countermeasures: he decided to launch his units to assault north, on both sides of the Bol.Dubovizy road, to drive the enemy back, before he could consolidate the conquered positions. *3.Kp./FD* attacked on the left side of the road and *2.Kp./FD* on the right. The *1.Kompanie* had to remain in reserve to be engaged on the western flank of the attack line, the most vulnerable area for an enemy threat. Two anti-tank pieces of the *4.Kompanie* were assigned as reinforcements to the *1.Kompanie.* Once the *Frikorps* broke through the Soviet lines, a *Totenkopf-Division* company, with three assault guns, would support the creation of a new defensive line.

At 6:30 on June 11, the battle began with a close duel between opposing artillery: the German batteries, located south-east of Vassiljevschtschina, confronted the Soviet batteries, located north of Bol.Dubovizy and east of the River Pula. As a result, Danish companies found themselves attacking without adequate artillery support, greatly delaying their forward progression. The fire of the Soviet field guns in fact hindered the movements of the Danish grenadiers and the German batteries were able to do little to counter it. Advancing for about five hundred meters in open field, overcoming great resistance, the Danish volunteers managed to reach the first houses of Bol Dubovizy, engaging in a very hard battle: every house had been transformed by the Soviets into a

SS-Obersturmführer **Per Sörensen.**

***SS-Ostuf.* Harald Boy-Hansen (*Lars Larsen*).**

fortress and every leap forward of the Danes was blocked by massive barrage fire unleashed by the Soviets while furious hand-to-hand clashes also raged. Meanwhile, the *1.Kompanie* of Sörensen and the *3.Kompanie* of Nielsen attempted to penetrate the village, while the *2.Kompanie* of Boy-Hansen, advanced along the western flank of the same, encountering strong resistance there too. *SS-Ostuf.* Boy-Hansen sighted an large concentration of enemy forces in the woods further west, a sign that the Soviets were about to counterattack.

After about two hours of furious struggle between the houses of Bol.Dubovizy, the *1.* and *3.Kp.* had managed to regain only a third of the position, but around 10:00, the expected Soviet counterattack was unleashed. The *2.Kompanie* found itself in the worst situation, since the Soviets exerted the greatest effort on the western flank: initially the Danish company managed to hold its positions, but when the enemy pressure intensified and especially when *SS-Ostuf.* Boy-Hansen fell under enemy fire, the men began to fall back in great disorder, south and south-east, leaving the side of the companies that were in the village exposed. In the furious battle that broke out inside Bol Dubovizy, the commander of the *3.Kp., S-Ustuf.* Nielsen fell. From the General Staff of the *Frikorps, SS-Ostuf.* Christen-Madsen Brodersen was sent to replace him. At 11:20 am, the first elements of the Soviet force gathered in the woods struck the western part of the village, hitting the Danes in the flank.

At 11:30, *SS-Stubaf.* von Lettow-Vorbeck ordered a general retreat. The *3.Kompanie* covered the maneuver, under severe pressure from the north and southwest. Von Lettow-Vorbeck, was just behind *3.Kp.* to direct the fighting: he had already been wounded twice, but he had decided to continue to remain on the front line. Thanks to his quick decisions and his presence in the middle of the action, it was possible to save the situation and the Danish companies from certain annihilation.

soldiers respond to enemy fire by staying well sheltered behind an abandoned cart.

Soviet infantry attack, supported by machine gun fire.

Committing his last forces, *SS-Ostuf.* Brodersen and his *3.Kompanie* succeeded in blocking the violent enemy attack. Per Sörensen's *1.Kompanie* was on the verge of being surrounded, so von Lettow-Vorbeck informed *SS-Ostuf.* Brodersen that he would go personally to bring help. The commander of the *Frikorps* and his liaison officer then left the positions of the *3.Kp.* and they set out.

A Danish *SS-Unterscharführer* in combat.

German infantry units raiding the Demyansk area, June 1942.

After traveling a few meters, they came under fire from Soviet machine guns and were killed. *Frikorps Danmark* had tragically lost its new commander. The last words of von Lettow-Vorbeck, immediately after being shot, were for his soldiers: "... *salute my brave Danes for me!*".

In his book on Freikorps, Martinsen described that tragic day: "... *the price paid was high. The commander fell, having been wounded several times that day. Two company commanders followed him and a large number of our comrades.*"

SS-Hstuf. Martinsen, once again, was called to take command of the Legion. After directing the heavy weapons fire of *4.Kompanie*, he had the men pull back in good order. Despite strong Soviet pressure, the Danes managed to recover von Lettow-Vorbeck's body and transport it to the command post of the Legion.

Towards noon, the Danish units again went back to their starting positions, together with the *Totenkopf* Motorcycle Battalion.

The attack against Bol.Dubovizy had cost the Danish Legion 59 casualties, including the unit commander and two company commanders. More than fifty were injured and some died in the field hospital from serious injuries. In total, the *Frikorps* had lost a quarter of its strength. The three rifle companies engaged directly in the fighting were left with about forty troops each. Only the *4.Kompanie* remained relatively fully staffed. That same evening, the Danish volunteers abandoned their positions, leaving them to the SS motorcyclists, marching in the direction of Vassiljevschtschina, located further west.

A group of Danish volunteers on the Demyansk front.

The arrival of the units of logistics services

While the *Frikorps* reached the front, its transport column, the field kitchen and the supply platoon were left behind, as it had not been possible to transport them by air with the rest of the units. On June 5, 1942, all these elements, under the orders of *SS-Hstuf.* Thorgils(2), began their journey from Rastenburg, East Prussia, to Demyansk, first by train and then by road. Meanwhile, *Frikorps* depended on *Totenkopf* for its logistical needs. On June 7, the logistical elements of the Legion arrived in Riga and on 9 June, in Staraya Russa, the nerve center of supplies for the German troops surrounded in the Demyansk salient. A number of German depots, mostly guarded by Russian auxiliaries, were located in the bombed-out buildings of the city.

Resting in the woods area are Poul Windekilde (right) and Jens Andreas Kristensen (centre) with an unknown comrade (*Lars Larsen Collection*).

During the night between 9 and 10 June, the men of the logistic services of the *Frikorps* were severely hit by the fire of the enemy mortars in their quarters. The field kitchen took

There was a lot of mud along the *Rollbahn* (*Larsen*).

A truck of the *Frikorps Danmark* went off the road.

Danish volunteers take a break (*Lars Larsen*).

a direct hit and several men were killed. Around 11 pm on June 10, the convoy with the logistical elements set out to cover the last and most difficult fifty kilometers that separated them from the *Frikorps* positions. The column traveled on a log road built by the pioneers between the swamps and immense quagmires of the Russian plain. At a certain point, they ended up under enemy fire and also for the rest of the journey, the men were always on alert. The linkup with the rearguard services of the *Frikorps* took place in Ramuschevo, on the western bank of the River Lovat. At that moment a new obstacle arose: the pontoon bridge over the river was badly damaged and the Soviets had placed floating mines on the water. The only possibility to cross the river remained the armed rafts that patrolled the river. This meant that the heavy trucks, as well as the field kitchen, had to be abandoned. And so it was that the Danish volunteers crossed the river without their heavy equipment.

The situation of the Frikorps

During the night of June 11, the first part of the logistical elements, under the orders of *SS-Uscha.* Leuschakke, finally reached the command post of the Legion. All the others arrived the next day. The positions of the *Frikorps* at that time were about three kilometers northwest of Vassiljevschtschina, where new entrenchments were being prepared in the wooded

***SS-Sturmbannführer* Knud Børge Martinsen.**

Sailing in a dinghy on the streams of Robja (*Lars Larsen*).

marshes. Two rifle companies each held a front of about one kilometer, while a third was in reserve. On that same June 12, *SS-Hstuf.* Bonnek(3) assumed command of the *2.Kompanie*. *SS-Hstuf.* Martinsen was promoted to the rank of *Sturmbannführer* and made effective commander of the *Frikorps*. At that moment, he was particularly busy deploying the heavy weapons of *4.Kompanie*, whose limited range did not allow them to directly hit the Soviet lines, located 2,500 meters away. The Legion's engineer platoon, left with only 14 men, was preparing new defensive positions, laying mines in the nearby marshes as well as having to build a new corduroy road for the transfer of the field kitchen and signals trucks. *SS-Hstuf.* Windig-Christensen(4), an engineer officer in the Legion's General Staff, was placed in command of the engineer platoon, replacing *SS-Ustuf.* Nils Faalgard, who fell in combat on the Robja River.

On June 18, 1942, the *Frikorps* signals platoon finally arrived at the front, after its members had finished training at the *Waffen SS* Signals School in Posen-Treskau. *Totenkopf* sent some of its *Flak* pieces to the Legion to ensure that it had a minimum of air protection. In the meantime, the situation had stabilized: patrols were sent during the night and contact with the nearby *Totenkopf* motorcyclists on the right was maintained. The booby traps set up by the pioneers routinely caused losses to the enemy. Beginning in late June, the Soviets began broadcasting loudspeaker messages to Danish lines, urging them to defect. These broadcasts were always followed by artillery bombardments.

SS-Hstuf. **Windig-Christensen.**

Prisoners of war carrying wouded and dead soldiers (*Jann Hornum*).

Soviet tanks destroyed.

On June 21, during one of these bombings, the commander of the *3. Kompanie, SS-Ostuf.* Brodersen, died. He was replaced by *SS-Hstuf.* Holger Windig-Christensen, who was himself injured on July 2. The command of *3./Frw.Leg.Danmark* was then assumed by *SS-Ostuf.* Heinz Henneke.

A new attack by the Soviets

On the evening of July 16, the news reached the *Frikorps* headquarters that a new massive Soviet attack was imminent. *Stubaf.* Martinsen immediately alerted his units. The *1.* and *3.Kp.*, plus a platoon of the *2.Kp.*, were transferred to the front line. The first company numbered 2 officers, 5 non-commissioned officers and 65 soldiers. The other rifle companies had more or less the same strengths. On the main defensive line, there were a total of 150 men, practically one soldier for every fifteen meters of the front. The day of the 17th began with a radiant sun and a 'strange' calm. Danish volunteers began to transfer large quantities of ammunition to the front line. About a thousand meters from the front line, the field kitchen was preparing lunch and groups of soldiers in its vicinit, ate and chatted. At exactly 12:30, without any warning, the Soviets opened fire with all their available weapons: artillery, mortars, 'Stalin's organs' and even tank guns. The whole area of Vassiljevschtschina was completely shaken by enemy fire.

Martinsen recalls the facts as follows: "*... on July 17th, it began with an apparent calm. Shortly after 12:00, when absolute calm reigned, a preparatory artillery fire went into action, with a force like never seen before, such was its strength and its duration* ". The shells began to fly over the Danish field kitchen and the cook and his assistants ran for cover quickly to save their skins. The earth shook under the impact of the numerous shells. The destructive fire continued for more than an hour. Telephone communications were lost, two radio stations remained active but the connections with the command post were in any case lost. The artillery observation posts had been destroyed and no one was able to direct the fire anymore. *SS-Stubaf.* Martinsen was therefore unable to get a precise idea of the situation: his command post was well camouflaged, but he did not have a good view of the battlefield.

On the left with a pipe is Niels K. Jensen, who was killed on 11 July 1942 (*Lars Larsen*).

Danish volunteers in a captured position with Russian heavy machine-gun *'Maxim Gorki'*.

When the artillery fire ended, the Soviet assault began: large masses of riflemen and groups of tanks advanced against the Danish positions and nothing seemed to stop them.

Defense to the bitter end

The companies on the front line, which survived the terrible hurricane of fire, tried to resist as best they could. The main attack began west of the Pola River: the companies of *Inf.Rgt.501* of the *209.Inf.Div.* in defense of that sector, had been completely overwhelmed and immediately afterwards Vassiljevschtschina and part of the supply line were also captured by the Soviets. Southwest of Vassiljevschtschina itself, *Jäger-Regiment 28* of the *8. Jäger-Div.* attempted to form a new defensive line, while the first Soviet tanks were advancing towards Biakovo.

SS-Untersturmführer **Egill Poulsen from** *2.Kp./FD.*

German 3,7 cm ***Pak 35/36*** **of a** ***Waffen SS*** **unit in firing position on the Eastern Front, 1942.**

Right there, a *Frikorps* anti-tank battery was in position, under the orders of *SS-Uscha.* Kunze, stationed in a nearby cornfield. A first *T-34* was hit and knocked out, but another came, from another location, which forced the Danish soldiers to have to move their gun. However, the Soviet tank was faster and at the last moment, the anti-tank crews had to jump into a ditch along the way to avoid being killed. The Soviet tank threw itself against the anti-tank gun, crushing it under its tracks.

The Soviet advance continued to progress along the railway line to the southeast, to exploit the terrain with greater effectiveness throughout the area. The Soviet forward elements reached the command post of *Jg.Rgt.28,* near which most of the German artillery batteries still intact were located. Firing at a short distance at the Soviet tanks, the German gunners managed to block their advance. Another Soviet armored spearhead instead pushed precisely against the positions of the *Frikorps.*

SS-Stubaf. Martinsen, described the situation as follows: "*... our neighbors on the right had withdrawn, leaving a breach of about three kilometers open. With all the left flank open, the* 1.Kompanie *retreated towards the railway line, where it joined two platoons of the 2.Kompanie and some elements of the staff*".

A group of Soviet *T-34* during an attack, 1942.

German soldiers marching along the railways line.

Danish volunteer in combat, July 1942.

In the course of the afternoon, the Soviets attempted to pass through the Danish positions. *SS-Ostuf.* Sörensen and *SS-Hstuf.* Bonnek counterattacked several times, to relieve enemy pressure, employing all available men. *SS-Stubaf.* Martinsen, who was unaware of the general situation, continued to deploy his forces letting himself be guided by intuition: towards the west, the *3. Kompanie* went to occupy the barrier positions, while the bulk of the *Freikorps* and all its reserves concentrated along the railway line further east. When the situation of the Danish Battalion was requested over the radio, Martinsen was able to report: "*... the Frikorps firmly holds its positions*". The *1.Kompanie* of *Ostuf.* Sörensen, left with forty men in total, was holding good positions in the eastern part of the old defensive line. Due to the swampy terrain, the Soviet tanks could not attack at that point, so that when they reached about four hundred meters from the Danish positions, they began firing high-explosive shells. Soon after, Soviet artillery also went into action, as the enemy infantry was regrouping to launch another assault. Sörensen divided his men into two platoons, displacing one to the west, under the orders of *SS-Ustuf.* Andersen and the other to the east, under the orders of *SS-Uscha.* Jens Nielsen. In the rear, he was left with some of his best soldiers, to be engaged in an emergency. Five machine guns covered the

A *Stuka* during an attack.

SS-Ostuf. Per Sörensen (*Larsen*).

A Soviet *T-34* destroyed, 1942.

defensive line. A long time passed and the wait began to become unnerving, however the enemy was nowhere to be seen. Taking advantage of the lull, the men were busy repairing the telephone line in an attempt to re-establish contact with the headquarters. Being surprised by the inactivity of the enemy, *SS-Ostuf.* Sörensen carried out a reconnaissance with his reserve group, but without obtaining any information. The Danish officer was under the impression that the Soviets were waiting for the Danes to drop their guard to attack. Increasingly worried, he then decided to call the command post, reporting to Martinsen his doubts about the ability of his company to withstand a strong enemy attack. Martinsen in turn called the command of the Army Corps to ask for the intervention of the *Stukas,* to hit the concentrations of Soviet troops. German dive bombers appeared that same evening, flying over the Soviet positions and dropping their deadly cargo on top of them, blowing up men, tanks and guns. The Soviet concentration in front of the positions of *1. Kompanie* was completely annihilated thus removing the threat. But the truce did not last long, as soon as it began to get dark, the threat of an enemy assault reappeared again: eight Soviet tanks advanced against the right wing of *1.Kompanie,* starting from the northwestern part of Vassiljevschtschina, firing their cannons and machine guns. Unable to reach the Danish positions due to the marshy terrain, they sent the infantry forward. A fierce hand-to-hand fight over the positions of the *1.Kompanie* immediately broke out, which lasted until midnight, when all the attackers were killed or thrown back. To take revenge for the setback suffered, the Soviets again called in their artillery.

Men versus tanks

In the early afternoon of July 17, it was the turn of *4.Kompanie* to face a new enemy attack: a Soviet infantry battalion, preceded by a single tank, advanced towards the village on both sides of the railway line, investing part of the positions of the

Danish company. In fact, some elements of the company, four pieces of light artillery, were located in a sparsely wooded area two kilometers west of Vassiljevschtschina and about three hundred meters from the railway line. This group was completely unaware of the situation, having lost contact with the battalion command post.

Danish volunteers firing with an *MG-34*, July 1942.

***Waffen-SS* soldier with a 7,5 cm *le.IG 18*.**

A first hint of impending danger was given by *SS-Uscha.* Kunze and the crews of his anti-tank unit, when they reported to the commander of *4.Kompanie*, *SS-Ostuf.* Stenger[(5)], on how they had lost their gun. Stenger immediately ordered his gunners to move their pieces along the railway line, to put them in firing position. The guns were oriented towards the east while an infantry platoon, under the orders of *SS-Oscha.* Berger, stood north of the railway line where he could establish contact with *2.Kompanie*. This made it possible to re-establish contact with the command post of the *Frikorps* and thus *SS-Stubaf.* Martinsen was informed of the imminent danger facing the *4.Kompanie*. The weak point of the defense was represented by Berger's infantry platoon, which numbered

A soviet tank destroyed by a *Pak 38* 50mm.

A Danish volunteer firing with a *Mauser* rifle.

A Danish defensive position with an *MG-34*.

only fourteen men, armed only with rifles and without machine guns. Although the uneven terrain severely limited the field of vision, the Danish volunteers managed to spot the enemy in time. The Soviet battalion, after the support tank became stuck, continued to advance in no particular order. At the same time, three other Soviet tanks were spotted moving in single file along the railway line. As soon as the Soviet infantrymen were taken in their sights by the Danish riflemen, they opened fire, forcing them to seek shelter. The tanks for their part continued to advance until they realized they had lost their supporting infantry. For the Danes, the situation was becoming increasingly critical: the last anti-tank piece of the *Frikorps*, a 50mm Pak, was located much further west. The four light guns were not suitable for countering the T-34s, but a Danish gun chief wanted to try it anyway, moving his piece along the railway embankment, immediately starting to fire. At first, fate was on his side, as the first shot managed to hit the Soviet tank in a vulnerable spot, putting it out of action. The other shots instead literally bounced off the armor of the other tanks, without causing any damage. The Soviet tanks opened fire in turn against the Danish gun, hitting it and killing all of the crew. The Danish riflemen, sheltered in the nearby woods, held their breath, thinking they were the next target, but luckily for them, they were wrong. *SS-Ostuf.* Stenger then moved his last three guns and his last two machine guns further east. The men of *4.*

Kompanie were reinforced with personnel from the field kitchen, assistants, supply personnel and whoever else was available and in this way the positions were held. At 19:00, the Soviets attacked again with another infantry battalion, still following the route of the railway line: this time the tanks provided long-range support fire. The three light infantry guns of the *4.Kompanie* immediately started firing as well as the two machine guns which hit the Soviet column with a crossfire. Within half an hour, the attack was over, with heavy losses for the Soviets. SS-*Oscha.* Degen, a platoon leader in the *4.Kompanie,* gathered all the men around him to cover the breaches south of the railway line, making contact with *2.Kompanie.* Over the course of the night, the Danish volunteers reinforced their defenses to prepare for the new enemy attacks. Meanwhile, *SS-Ostuf.* Dr. Lotze, the battalion's medical officer, was always busy helping the many wounded. The main field hospital, located in Vassiljevschtschina, was overcrowded due to the impossibility of transferring the wounded to Biakovo and Ramuschevo. Between midnight and 4:00 on 18 July, the sector remained absolutely quiet, then after 4:00 all hell broke out again: artillery and tanks opened fire on the Danish positions before the infantry assault. The companies of *SS-Ostuf.* Sörensen, of *SS-Ostuf.* Stenger and of *SS-Hstuf.* Bonnek held their positions and frustrated the Soviet efforts. Around noon, *SS-Stubaf.* Martinsen called Sörensen to find out about the situation of his company: "*... the situation appears complicated, but we will defend our positions until the last man,*" replied the officer. Martinsen told his company commanders that there were no more reserves and they had to make do as best they could. The only thing he could do was to try to get in touch with the command post of *Jg.Rgt.28,* through a mounted runner, to look for reinforcements. Passing literally through the Soviet lines, the runner was able to get a company as reinforcement, with reduced manning, from the *30. Infanterie-Division.* This unit, under the orders of *Leutnant* Fortmann, reported to the *Frikorps* command post immediately after, receiving the order to deploy on the defensive line between *1.* and *3.Kp./FD. III./Jg.Rgt.28* also arrived as a reinforcement and took up positions behind the defensive line as a reserve force. During the night of July 18, *SS-Stubaf.* Martinsen and the commander of *III./Jg.Rgt.28* discussed the operational plans for the next day: it was decided that the *Frikorps* would maintain a defensive attitude, while the German battalion would attack on both sides of the railway line in the direction of Vassiljevschtschina. The forward artillery observers of *4.Kp./Fr.Danmark,* were then attached to the German battalion in order to better direct the fire of their light infantry guns.

Notes

(1) Hans v. Lettow-Vorbeck, born April 28, 1901 in Berlin, SS-Nr. 203 005. Previously he was in command of *5./'Germania'.*

(2) Knud Thorgils, born on 8 July 1906 in Slagelse in Denmark.

(3) Dirck-Ingvard Bonnek, born August 20, 1909 in Ramstrup, Denmark.

(4) Holger-Winding Christensen, born on 22 August 1902 in Fredericia in Denmark.

(5) Helmut Stenger, born on 9 June 1917 in Fechtingen, SS-Nr. 270 046. Previously he served in the *13./Tot.Inf.Rgt.3* (1940) and in the *2./Flak-Abt. 'Totenkopf'* (1942).

Bibliography

M. Afiero,"*Frikorps Danmark: i volontari danesi sul fronte dell'Est, 1941-1943*", Ass. Cult. Ritterkreuz

Jens Pank Bjerregaard, Lars Larsen, "*Danish Volunteers of the Waffen-SS: Freikorps Danmark 1941-43*", Helion & Co Ltd

Walloon volunteers in the German armed forces

By Massimiliano Afiero

Part 2

The Walloons of *Oberfeldwebel* Lassois attempted to approach Soviet positions, but ended up under enemy fire, suffering dead and wounded. After placing themselves under cover of some sheaves of straw, the Walloon legionaries managed to approach the enemy positions, among the ruins of the villages of Iablenskaïa and Nikolaïevka, and then attack them, thanks also to the support fire of the German artillery.

May 1942: *Hauptmann* Tchekhoff and *Oberfeldwebel* Lassois inspecting Walloon volunteers at Brachowka (*Dernier Carré – Léon Degrelle*).

Furious hand-to-hand combat followed without mercy. Despite the losses, the conquest of Iablenskaïa and Nikolajewka was a great military success. In the afternoon, the march resumed to chase the fleeing enemy. The Wallonie Legion headed for the Donetz, covering some fifty kilometers, with unbearable heat. On May 19, the Walloons arrived in Prelesnoïe, where they stayed for a few days, before resuming the march on May 26, 1942, to reach Brachowka.

Reinforcements come

While the Walloons were fighting on the Eastern front, in Belgium the enlistment campaign for the Legion had continued. Thanks above all to the propaganda action of

Victor Matthys, leader of the Rex movement in the absence of Degrelle and to the work of Jean Vermeire, sent on mission to his homeland by Pauly, 363 new volunteers, 333 soldiers, twenty-six non-commissioned officers and four officers were recruited. Most of the new volunteers came from the Rexist youth led by their leader, John Hagemans. In March 1942, 150 young people aged between 16 and 18 followed him without hesitation.

Belgian nationalist group the Rexist Party is seen here on parade in Brussels in 1942, with the new flags for the Walloon Legion (U.S. NARA).

John Hageman with German uniform on the Eastern Front, Spring 1942 (*Hugh Page Taylor*).

To these Jeunesse boys joined another 150 new volunteers, slightly older and about sixty wounded from Gromowaja-Balka, recovered. The young volunteers who joined the Wallonie Legion brought with them four company banners and a battalion flag. Designed by Hagemans himself, these emblems represented Burgundy Cross, red on a white background. Followed by his faithful assistant, Roger De Goy, John Hagemans participated in the last parade on the *La Grand-Place* in Brussels. Then, the new volunteers left for Meseritz training camp to receive the necessary training. The new reinforcements included 360 men, divided into two companies: the 6th, which brought together young people and the 7th, which brought together the 'elderly', those who were over twenty

Leutnant **Jean Vermeire (*Hugh Page Taylor*).**

Hauptmann **Lucien Lippert (*U.S. NARA*).**

years old. At the head of the 6th, was placed *Leutnant* Jean Vermeire, and at the head of the 7th, *Leutnant* Henri Thyssen. On June 2, 1942, the train with these new volunteers arrived in Slaviansk. To welcome them, Léon Degrelle, who after haranguing them with one of his speeches, led them to Brachowka. The Walloon battalion at that time occupied defensive positions along the Donetz, on a front of about four kilometers. The commander of the legion decided to distribute the new volunteers among the various companies to strengthen them and reconstitute the second company. At the same time, new support units were created: a *Pak* platoon with pieces pulled by half-tracks, under the orders of *Oberfeldwebel* Pierre Dengis and a pioneer platoon under the orders of *Oberfeldwebel* Mirgain. In addition, the *Tross*, the Legion's logistic train, was reinforced by a platoon of *Hiwis,* Russian auxiliary volunteers. The battalion now had 850 Walloon legionnaires and a hundred Russian volunteers. A new commander was also appointed following Degrelle's personal proposal, *Oberleutnant* Lucien Lippert(1) was chosen, despite his modest rank and his young age.

Legion Order of battle June 1942

Commander: *Oberleutnant* Lucien Lippert
Staff: *Leutnant* Lassois, *Leutnant* Degrelle
Medical services: *Oberleutnant* Dr. Jacquemin, *Leutnant* Dr. Albert
German liaison officer: *Rittmeister* von Rabenau
1.Kompanie: *Leutnant* Mathieu
2.Kompanie: *Leutnant* Vermeire
3.Kompanie: *Leutnant* Ruelle
4.Kompanie: *Leutnant* Bosquion

Operational area of the Walloon Legion between May and July 1942.

Degrelle, Lippert and German officers, Summer 1942.

Towards the Caucasus

With the beginning of the German offensive towards the Caucasus (*Fall Blau*), the Walloon Legion always under control of the *97.Jäger Division,* leaving its positions at Spaschowska and occupying the position of Kamenka. On the evening of June 22, 1942, Walloon volunteers crossed the Donetz south of Izjum, and then marched towards Kupiansk. On the afternoon of June 24, the Walloon units arrived in Kapitanowska, three kilometers east of Izjum, restoring connections with the units of the *97.Jäger Division.* On June 26, the Walloons reached Shurki (Churki), a small village north-west of Slavjansk. On July 4th, General Rupp, commander of the *97.Jäger-Division,* distributed some Iron Crosses Second Class to the soldiers who had distinguished themselves in previous fighting. On July 7, 1942, the Walloon Legion resumed the march following the German armies of the Army Group A, towards the Caucasus. In the night between 10 and 11 July, the Walloons crossed the Donetz, to then reach Torskaïa. In the morning, they resumed their march, in pursuit of the retreating Soviet troops. On July 24, the Walloon Battalion crossed the Don River to Melekhovskaja. Two days later the Walloons arrived on the banks of the Manytsch river, the river that marked the border between Europe and Asia. The Wallonie Legion continued its march and on August 4, the Kuban was reached. After crossing the river, the Walloons headquartered in Armavir. After a day of rest, they left for Labinskaïa,

Degrelle and Walloon volunteers marching during the offensive into the Caucasus in the summer of 1942 (NARA).

Summer 1942, Walloon volunteers on the march (*Dernier Carré – Léon Degrelle*).

placing themselves at the forefront of the *97.Jäger-Division*. On August 13, after a few days of forced marches and travelling about eight hundred kilometers in hellish heat, the Walloons entered at Maikop. On the night between 14 and 15 August 1942, the Walloon Legion resumed its march with the Black Sea shores as its ultimate goal. The commander of the *97.Jäger-Division*, having to ensure control of a large sector, was forced to divide his forces in two combat groups: *Jäger-Regiment 204* headed west, towards Tuapse, while *Kampfgruppe Ott*, comprising *Jäger-Regiment 207*, under the orders of the *Oberst* Ernst-Ludwig Ott, and the *Wallonie*, instead continued in the direction of Adler on the Black Sea. The Walloon units penetrated the mountains of the Caucasus. The two *Kampfgruppen* initially encountered little resistance, chasing the Soviet forces that beat in retreat. *Kampfgruppe Ott* in three days of march advanced about 150 kilometers. The Soviets, however, were lying in wait and patrols of enemy soldiers and partisans had been spotted everywhere. And so it was that the General Staff of the *97.Jäger-Division*, which marched in the center of the two *Kampfgruppen*, remained surrounded in the village of Schirwanskaja.

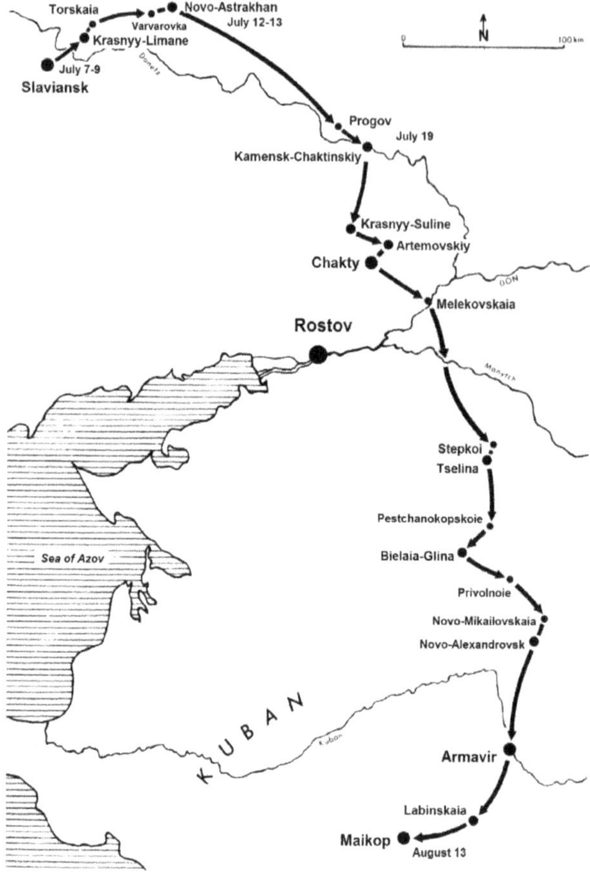

Advance of the Walloon legion in the Caucasian region, Summer 1942.

Degrelle and Walloon volunteers in combat.

The Walloon legionaries were then ordered to free their comrades from the *Wehrmacht*. At dawn on August 19, the men of the Dumont company and the machine gunners of the Bosquion company successfully attacked the village of Prusskaïa first and then established the connection with the units surrounded in Schirwanskaja, fleeing the enemy forces.

The Battle for Tjerjakow

On August 21, 1942, the Walloons resumed their march to south: the battalion was ordered to divide its forces to better rake this region, that was so difficult to control. And so, while *Leutnant* Closset went on a reconnaissance with his second company, the other three companies, with *Leutnant* Dumont, Ruelle and Bosquion, received the order to attack the village of Tjerjakow, anchored on a rocky spur, occupied by the Soviets. One part of the battalion was to attack and the other to remain in support. A platoon of the first company, under the orders of the *Oberfeldwebel* Foulon, went to the wooded hills on the right, trying to emerge on the side of the Soviets. The commander decided to commit all the Legion's heavy weapons: the machine guns of *Oberfeldwebel* Kehren, the mortars of *Oberfeldwebel* Graff and also the *Pak* of *Oberfeldwebel* Dengis.

Lucien Lippert and Léon Degrelle in the Caucasian region, Summer 1942.

Autumn 1942, Northwest Caucasus: Léon Degrelle during the ceremony for the delivery of decorations.

The Walloon legionaries launched the attack with incredible dash, climbing the slopes of the rocky spur, breaking through the doors of the houses and knocking out the defenders of Tjerjakow. Within minutes, the village fell into their hands. But a few hours later, the Soviets counterattacked, initially investing the third company of Ruelle, which had taken a position in the local *Kolkhoz*. Thanks to the support of heavy weapons, the enemy assault was repelled. Throughout the night, the Soviets continued to launch attacks to attempt to recapture the village and *Kolkhoz*. The following morning, the Soviets returned to attack, this time however moving from the forest, behind the village. But they were still repulsed. A few hours later, a new attack moved the fighting inside the village, characterized by furious clashes. Tjerjakow turned into hell: the Walloon legionaries continued to fight fiercely, sustaining heavy losses. Only when they managed to eliminate the fire positions of enemy heavy weapons did the situation stabilize. Soviet units retreated to the forest again and no longer launched attacks on Tjerjakow. In the following days, the Walloons were mainly engaged in maintaining contact with the other German units in the sector, sending patrols ahead. Just during the action of one of these patrols, Sergeant John Hagemans, the leader of the Rexist youth, fell in combat. At the end of the battle for Tjerjakow, Commander Lippert was decorated with the Iron Cross First Class, Léon Degrelle with the Infantry Assault Badge and eleven other legionaries with the Iron Cross Second Class. On August 28, the Walloon units were taken over by those of *Wiking* in

Oberleutnant **Degrelle, carrying the insignia of the German mountain troops, the metal edelweiss, on the left of the cap.**

Tjerjakow. The next day, the bulk of the battalion left for Kubano-Armiansk, east of Tjerjakow, where the second company of *Leutnant* Closset was already located.

The end of the campaign in the Caucasus

Throughout the month of September, the Walloons were engaged only in reconnaissance actions, always sending out patrols. With the beginning of October, rain and mud returned. The Germans wanted to get to Tuapse before winter. The offensive resumed in the upper Piscisc valley. On the evening of October 6, 1942, the Wallonie legion left the village of Kubano-Armiansk, to follow the *97.Jäger-Division*. Under incessant rain, the Walloons marched on difficult mountain paths, encountering considerable difficulties. Until mid-October, the legionaries continued to engage in small operations without achieving any significant results. The legion then descended into the Pscisc valley, then went up again to occupy surveillance positions on the surrounding ridges. Twenty kilometers as the crow flies, there was the city of Tuapse. From October 22, the legionaries occupied a defensive position south of Navajinski. With the arrival of the Autumn, the situation worsened further for the legionnaires, complaining of new losses especially for health reasons. At the beginning of November, the legion reduced to just 187 men, was definitively withdrawn from the front line, following the withdrawal of the German armies from the Caucasus following the worsening of the situation on the Stalingrad front. The Walloons received received three weeks home leave. As a sign of recognition for the employment with the *97.Jäger Division*, veterans of the Caucasus campaign had the privilege of carrying the insignia of the German mountain troops, the metal edelweiss, on the left of the cap and the cloth arm badge, an oval also with the Edelweiss, on the right sleeve of the uniform. On the Eastern front, also in the Caucasian regions, a hundred volunteers belonging to the second contingent remained, under the orders of *Leutnant* Léon Closset, still attached to the *97.Jäger-Division*. These elements participated in the rearguard fighting for the evacuation of the German units from the Caucasus, being then transferred by air to Crimea in February 1943.

Bibliography

M. Afiero, "*Belgian Waffen-SS Legion & Brigade 1941–44*", Osprey Publishing
M. Afiero, "*Rex Vaincra: Leon Degrelle e la Legione Wallonie*", Soldiershop Publishing
M. Afiero, "*Wallonie*", Marvia Edizioni
E. de Bruyne e M. Rikmenspoel, "*For Rex and for Belgium*", Helion & Company
L. Degrelle, "*Fronte dell'Est*", editrice Sentinella d'Italia
J. Mabire, "*Légion Wallonie au front de l'Est 1941-44*", Presses de la Cité

The Hird Special Unit: the origins of Førergarden (1 February to 19 April 1942)

by Hugh Page Taylor

Uranienborg school in 2018. Photograph courtesy Fiona Bell

The exact date the decision was taken to provide Quisling with a full-time paramilitary bodyguard when he became Minister President is not known. What is certain is that at first there was a degree of confusion regarding the name that bodyguard should have. As will be seen below, it is important to note that the name *Førergarden*, the Leader's Guard, was not adopted on the day Quisling was appointed Norway's Minister President by the so-called "Act of State" (*statsakten*) on 1 February 1942. Before that final name was adopted at Quisling's own request in mid-May 1942, a number of transitional titles, not all of which were formally recognised, were adopted and subsequently abandoned. Before the name Førergarden was adopted, a rather confused and confusing transitional period had to pass. From the very start members of the National *Hird*, who had either volunteered or been selected for what was to be full-time duty (unlike elsewhere in that organization), were barracked at the Uranienborg School close to the former Royal Palace in Oslo. Whether preparations for the creation of the unit had been made in advance, and/or steps taken in the days immediately following 1 February 1942 were deliberately back-dated to that date to make it coincide with Quisling's appointment is also a mystery, but it was and has been an over-simplification to say that a unit named Førergarden was formed on or immediately after 1 February 1942[1]. Throughout 1941 Quisling had strived to convince the Germans to allow Norway to have a national government — with him at its head — but he was only informed that this had been agreed on 17 January 1942. The effective date would have been the 30th of that month but, as it turned out, this had to be delayed by two days and instead occurred on 1 February 1942. Although it is likely that some steps were taken to plan for the unit's organization, such as coordinating its specific duties and perhaps commissioning uniforms and insignia in the days before 1 February 1942, no signs of new uniforms are to be seen in photographs or the official newsreels that documented the inaugural ceremony held on that day at the Akershus Fortress in Oslo. What in fact happened was that on 1 February 1942 and over the following days a number of *Hird* men volunteered or were selected to protect Quisling at his new office and

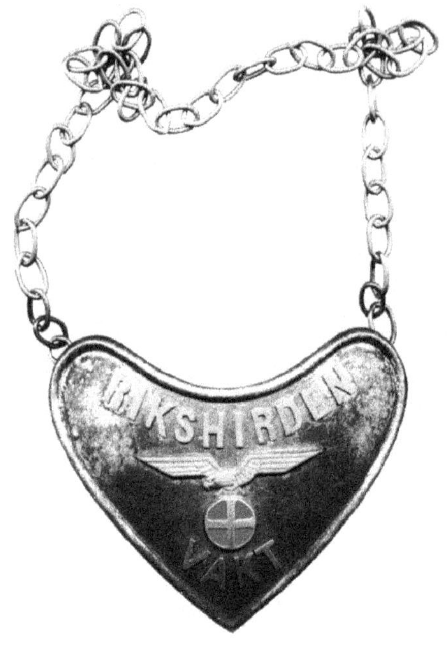

The duty gorget of the *Rikshird Vakt*. Gold lettering on a silver backing, with gold and red N.S. emblem, suspended by a chain or a leather strap attached to the reverse: *Nasjonal Samlings Metallmerker 1934-45*, page 52

A member of the *Hird* Guard wearing the duty gorget checks documents: *Nasjonal Samlings Metallmerker 1934-45*, page 52

headquarters in Oslo Palace. Some, if not all of them, were from the existing *Hird* guard (*Hirdvakt*), which at least one reliable source has called the *"Leader's Hird"* (*Førerhird*)[2]. In less than a week, a commander (or chief – *sjef*) was appointed and until 20 April 1942 there followed a provisional period during which the unit remained a part of the Hird. Its name was changed officially during that time from *"the Guard"* (*Garden*) to *"the Leader's Guard"* (*Førerens Garde*). Quisling had already been unpopular before the invasion as leader of *Nasjonal Samling* and was seen by most as a poor imitation of Hitler in Nazi Germany. However, the risk of attack if not assassination increased first when he was perceived to have aided and abetted with the Germans in their invasion of April 1940, and then even more so when they appointed him to be the Minister President of occupied Norway. To most Norwegians he was a lackey of the occupying enemy force and the ultimate form of traitor, a dubious distinction that would forever bear his name. He needed protection in not only Oslo – at his office and headquarters in Oslo Palace and at his official residence, Gimle in Bygdøy – but also when he travelled around Norway.

Before he became Minister President on 1 February 1942, Quisling's personal protection had been entrusted to a small unit of the Rikshird, known as the *"Hird Guard"* (*Hirdvakten*) or *"National Hird Guard"* (*Rikshirden Vakt*). It was made up of a select number of *Hird* men, all serving part-time, who provided Quisling with protection when at work in his office, at home and when attending meetings and rallies, as well as guarding the *Hird* H.Q. at Tollbodgaten 10 in central Oslo[3]. When on duty its men wore a gorget with the words "RIKSHIRDEN" and "VAKT" respectively above and below the N.S. eagle and sun cross with swords (solkorset med sverd). Quisling's new status as Minister President, however, and the greater risks to which this role exposed him, required a much higher and permanent level of protection on and after 1 February 1942. Rumours that such protection would have been provided by *Norges SS*, which had been formed on 21 May 1941 as the extension to Norway of the German General SS (*Allgemeine-SS*), turned out to be unfounded.

These two *Hird* members mount guard outside the *Rikshird*'s headquarters in Oslo, but do not wear the duty gorget, suggesting this photograph was taken before it was introduced, after its use had been discontinued, or that it was not worn at all times.

It has been suggested that Quisling's protection consisted of a 3-tier system, with the first tier made up of his adjutants who were closest to him, then the police, and finally the subject of this article, *Førergarden*, but that reconstruction is not entirely correct, at least insofar as the adjutants were concerned[4]. In fact, during his time as Minister President, Quisling had just two levels of personal protection. The first was provided by the police, who patrolled Oslo Palace where he worked and Gimle, his official residence in Bygdøy, and provided undercover protection while he travelled around the country. The second was his own highly conspicuous personal bodyguard that would later be named, at his request, *"the Leader's Guard"* or *Førergarden*. It was a relatively small but prestigious unit that evolved from humble beginnings on the very day Quisling was appointed Minister President of Norway on 1 February 1942. A considerable number of *Hird* members had been summoned to Oslo from all parts of the country to attend what they thought was to be a rally. In reality, its purpose was to add a semblance of historical importance and gravitas to Quisling's investiture at Akershus Fortress on 1 February 1942[5].

Nestregimentfører **Thorvald Thronsen, Chief of Staff of the National** ***Hird*** **(*****Stabsjef i Rikshirden*****), on 3 March 1943* at the opening of the** ***Hird*** **Officers School (*****Hirdførerskole*****) at Odnes, 83 miles (134 km) north of Oslo, with the leader of the Marine** ***Hird*** **(*****Hirdmarinesjef*****) Bertel Brun**.**

* 3 March is given in Munin, No. 4, April 1943, whereas 5 March in NS Årbok 1944, page 35, which states that the school was opened by Hirdsjef Møystad.

** Born on 12 September 1905, Brun served in the 5th Anti-Aircraft Battalion (*SS-Flak-Abteilung 5*) of the 5th SS "*Wiking*" Division, receiving the Iron Cross 2nd Class on 4 June 1942 by when he held the rank of *SS-Obersturmführer*. He died on 17 March 1987. The caption to this photograph mispelled both Thronsen (as Thronsen) and Brun (as Bruun).

A select number of the *Hird* stood inside the building along the side walls of the Knights' Hall where the ceremony took place under huge N.S. and Nazi eagles[6]. Others mounted guard outside the building together with members of the A.T. and police. Many more lined the approach road to the Fortress, the ear flaps of their caps turned down as the snow fell and the Norwegian and German dignitaries first arrived and then departed by car after the ceremony. All of these *Hird* men appear to have worn standard *Hird* uniforms without any special badges and certainly without any gorgets. A small select number of them would continue to provide protection to their leader in what was eventually to become known as *Førergarden*. Shortly before, 25-year old Thorvald Thronsen had returned to Oslo after a year's tour of duty on the Eastern Front in the "*Wiking*" Division of the *Waffen-SS* and had resumed his role as the National *Hird*'s Chief of Staff on 7 January 1942[7]. He appreciated and saw the need for Quisling to have a higher level of personal protection than before, not only at work and during the day at his office in Oslo Palace, outside of which on Slottsplasen angry crowds could be expected to gather and demonstrate, but also at rallies and meetings, in Oslo and around the country, and when off duty at home in his official and other residences. Thronen realised that the required high level of commitment could not be provided by well-trained but nonetheless part-time *Hird* members, even those who had served in the *Hird* Guard. Exactly when he came to this conclusion and why such an important matter should have been left up to him is not known, but Quisling held him in high regard and appreciated his initiative, as did his colleagues in the N.S. and the *Hird*. Consequently, Thronsen was authorized to go ahead and raise what would eventually be named *Førergarden*[8].

Thronsen in *Hird* uniform, but captioned as being an *SS-Obersturmführer*.

***Hird sveitfører* Rolf Gulbrandsen, who commanded Quisling's *Hird* bodyguard from 5 February to 20 April 1942: *Hirdmannen*, No. 6, 14 February 1942**

First, a suitable and reliable Hird officer had to be found to command such a unit, organize its duties at Oslo Palace and Gimle, and build it up to the required strength. It is not known if other candidates were approached but Thronsen invited sveitfører Rolf Gulbrandsen(9) from Oslo to the Hird HQ at Tollbodgaten 10 in the city center for an interview for the post. Gulbrandsen was then 35 years of age and head of the N.S. National Organizations Office (*kontorsjef i Riksorganisasjonen*). At that stage Thronsen appears only to have mentioned to him that the new unit's duty was to guard Quisling at the Palace, without making any reference to Gimle. The meeting went well and Thronsen chose Gulbrandsen, who accepted his appointment as chief (*sjef*) of the new unit with effect from 5 February 1942(10). The question therefore remains as to who was in charge of the guards in those first four days of February, given that guard duty is confirmed to have begun on the very day of Quisling's inauguration. A Hird officer must have been in command of the individual guards and this may have been Gulbrandsen before his formal appointment; alternatively 1 February may have been the formal date the unit was established, but in reality what had happened on the 5th may have been back-dated to coincide with the Akershus Act of State. To commemorate the second anniversary of the founding of the Reichskommissariat, a unique book was produced, in what is believed to have been just one original copy, entitled *Das zweite Jahr Reichskommissariat für die besetzten norwegischen Gebiete* (The Second Year of the Reich Commissariat for the occupied Norwegian Territories). This contains what may have been the first photograph of the *"special unit of the National Hird"* reproduced below, which has not been found published in any other periodical or book, contemporary or post-war.

Oslo Palace, early February 1942, possibly even the first day of the month: The original 15 members of the *Hird* Honor Guard at Oslo Palace march along the front of the Palace towards the guard house behind their leader, presumably Rolf Gulbrandsen. *Das zweite Jahr Reichskommissariat für die besetzten norwegischen Gebiete.* Author's collection

The caption reads *"A Hird battalion has taken over the Honor Guard at Oslo Palace, the Official Seat of the Minister President"*(11). This is misleading, however, as the German word *"Abteilung"* when applied to a military unit corresponds to a battalion, approximately 600 men, and in this photograph one can count three ranks of five men each and one leader, giving a total of just sixteen(12). The first mention of the new bodyguard in the press appeared in the Hird's own weekly newspaper, Hirdmannen, No. 5, 7 February 1942, which reported on events of two days before. It translates literally as follows:

The Leader's Guard (*Førerens garde*)

The Norwegian split flag now flies over the Palace after our Leader, Norway's Minister President, Vidkun Quisling, has established his headquarters there. We live in historic times, and last Thurdsday [i.e. 5 February 1942] a new page was added to our country's history. On that day the new cabinet held its first meeting, and on the same day a special unit of the national Hird (*spesialavdeling av Rikshirden*) took over the guard at the palace. A stout *Hird* man was posted on either side of the entrance, and when the ministers arrived, led by the Leader, the Leader's Guard stood guard on each side of the staircase up to the meeting room on the second floor. The chief of the guard is the former chief of the National Organizations Office (*kontorsjef i Riksorganisasjonen*), *sveitfører* Rolv Gulbrandsen, who in this case has taken on a very challenging task. The unit will consist of first-rate members of the *Hird* and will receive thorough and comprehensive training. After the meeting, the *Hird* paraded for the Leader in front of the Palace.

Oslo Palace, 5 February 1942: Quisling presides over the first meeting of the new Norwegian National Government.

Oslo Palace, 5 February 1942: *"Guard Chief"* (gardens sjef) *sveitfører* Rolf Gulbrandsen and what appears to be 10 of his men greet Quisling as he arrives for work at Oslo Palace: *Hirdmannen*, No. 5, 7 February 1942: Author's collection

The wording of this short article raises two issues that require clarification. First, if the *"special National Hird unit"* only began to guard the Palace on 5 February, then who had been doing so since Quisling transferred there four days before on the first of the month? The simple explanation appears to be an error in the article as other sources confirm that Quisling was driven by car to take up office in the Palace immediately after leaving Akershus Fortress on the afternoon of 1 February. The other point of interest was the premature use of the term *"Førerens garde"* as this was used generically and had not at that stage been adopted as the unit's formal title, which

HIRDMANNEN

3. årgang – Nr. 5. Kamporgan for Rikshirden og Norges Oslo, lørdag 7. februar 1942

Føreren tar roret!

Vår Fører, ministerpresident Vidkun Quislings tale til sine landsmenn 1. februar 1942

Våbenhird-bataljonen.

NORGES FREMTID

Førerens garde.

Cover of *Hirdmannen*, No. 5, 7 February 1942

was still being referred to as a "special unit" of the *Hird*. This short article appeared below a photograph that was most probably taken on 5 February 1942 and shows Gulbrandsen giving the Nazi salute as Quisling's limousine approached Oslo Palace. Ten *Hird* men can be seen behind Gulbrandsen, suggesting an incomplete lag, which was the smallest unit in the *Hird* made up of a leader (*lagfører*) and 11 men, thus 12 in all. The Karl Johan monument is seen top right, positioning Gulbrandsen and his men in front of the main entrance to the Palace. Much fuller coverage of the new guard unit at Oslo Palace followed in the next issue of *Hirdmannen*, No. 6, 14 February 1942. On the front cover was a photograph of a solitary Hird man on guard in front of his sentry box, next to one of the ornate lamp posts outside the Palace's front entrance, with a long police baton hanging from his belt. Most of page 2 is taken up with an article headed "*The National Hird has taken over the guard at Oslo Palace*":

THE NATIONAL *HIRD* HAS TAKEN OVER THE GUARD AT OSLO PALACE

The *Hird* guard at the Palace is becoming a permanent feature of Oslo's cityscape. Everyone who walks through the Palace Park stops to admire these handsome fellows who are guarding Norway's Leader. They take their duties seriously and we would not encourage anyone to try and get past them with their fearsome police batons. The sun shone and the split flag fluttered festively in the wind when we visited the guard house (*vaktstuen*) the other day. In front of the palace, children tumbled with bobsleds and kick-sleds, while the guards, straight-backed and serious, marched 13 steps forward and 13 steps back. The most courageous of the children dared to approach the silent guards in their blue uniforms. Soon they became more trusting, and with a child's instinct for safety, realized that they had nothing to fear from these handsome men. The *Hird* guard has now already secured high status among Norway's youngest, playing in the square in front of the Palace. The whole guard force is currently barracked at Uranienborg School. The main strength is divided into two guard forces, each of which serves for a continuous 24 hours. They keep uninterrupted guard day and night, every man at his post for 2 hours, after which he has 4 hours' rest.

Oslo Palace, 5 February 1942: A *Hird* guard with police baton outside the front entrance: *Hirdmannen*, No. 6, 14 Feb. 1942

HIRDMANNEN

3. årgang – Nr. 6 Kamporgan for Rikshirden og Norges SS Oslo, lørdag 14. februar 1942

Hirden er Norges ryggrad.

Nasjonal ungdomstjeneste.

En lov som vil få avgjørende betydning for NORGES FREMTID

INNSATS!

Cover of *Hirdmannen*, No. 6, 14 Feb. 1942

The main changing of the guard takes place every day at 2 p.m., with speed and precision, and always attracts a crowd of interested onlookers. Many of the public look on thoughtfully at the *Hird* men as they perform their duty with soldierly discipline and precision. Perhaps our opponents are beginning to realise the significance of Norwegian *Hird* men having taken over guard duty at Oslo Palace. We pay a visit to the guard house and chat with a number of the *Hird* men who are enjoying themselves and are stretched out on beds awaiting their turn. One cannot say that they are resting in luxurious surroundings. The old Palace guard house[13] is probably one of the ugliest and least cozy places one can imagine. But this will hopefully be taken care of. But despite the fact that the service is strict, the guard house is not very enjoyable, and the diet is as simple and lean as possible, the men are all excited about the honorable assignment they have been awarded. They fully appreciate the importance of the fact that the National *Hird* – Vidkun Quisling's *Hird* men – have taken over the guard at Oslo Palace. And when the trusted *Hird* man takes up position at his post in front of the Palace's great entrance in the dark and icy cold of the winter night, his chest is filled with warm enthusiasm because he – a *Hird* man – is entrusted with the guard because his Leader has his seat here as Norway's minister president and Head of State. The fight – the Leader's and the *Hird* men's battle and effort – has led him on inwardly, guarding the Leader, while the Leader guards all the people.

This article was illustrated with 5 photographs which, despite the poor newsprint quality, are worth reproducing for their historical importance. Unfortunately, all attempts to locate better prints have proven fruitless. According to *Hirdmannen*, No. 5, 29 January 1944, during his time in command from 5 February to 20 April 1942, Gulbrandsen's unit was known officially by just two names: first the simple "*Garden*" (the Guard) and then "*Førerens Garde*" (the Leader's Guard). While that may have been the official situation, several other names were used and have been found in contemporary documents.

Oslo Palace, February 1942: Changing the guard outside the Palace. Logically each group would have constituted a *lag* or *vaktlag*, made up of a lagfører and 11 men, so 12 each,* which would appear to have been the case insofar as the group at the left of this photograph is concerned, yet there seem to have been more — a *lagfører* and some 15 or so men — in the group at the right. If, as the text of the article suggests, the unit's strength was at that stage mainly two groups, then the total strength of the new guard unit would therefore have been between about 27 and 30 guards plus some administrative staff and so prior to the arrival of the 60 or so graduates from the Leira *Hird* School: *Hirdmannen*, No. 6, 14 February 1942.

*A Hird lag was made up of a *lagfører* and 11 *Hird* men (*Orvar Sæther: Hirdboken. Hirdens Historie og Oppgaver*, page 67, and Ekserserreglement for Rikshirden, Oslo, 1942, page 39).

These were more generic and thus used to describe the unit, rather than serve as its official title and those found so far are:

✓ *spesialavdeling av Rikshirden* (special unit of the National *Hird*): this was the earliest;
✓ *Hirdens honnørgarde* (the Hird's Honor Guard);
✓ *Garde for Føreren* (the guard for the Leader)(14);
✓ *Førerens Livgarde* (the Leader's Life Guard)(15);
✓ *Førervakt* (the Leader's Guard).

Liste. Nr. 1, the list hurriedly published in May 1945 to assist the post-war Norwegian police identify and track down suspected traitors, identified the unit by its final name, Førergarden, but also used no less than the following five other names for what clearly should have been Garden, Førerens Garde or Førergarden:

✓ *Quislings garde* (Quisling's guard);
✓ *Quislings livgarde* (Quisling's life guard)
✓ *Quislings livvakt* (Quisling's life guard);
✓ *Quislings vakt* (Quisling's guard);
✓ *Førervakten* (the Leader's Guard).

Oslo Palace, February 1942: A *Hird* man marches in front of the main entrance to the Palace with the Karl Johan monument behind him. *Hirdmannen*, No. 6, 14 February 1942

RIKSHIRDEN HAR OVERTATT vaktholdet ved Oslo slott.

Article in *Hirdmannen*, No. 6, 14 February 1942

None of these is believed to have been official and probably resulted from inaccurate and/or confused fact-finding and reporting. The Norwegian Resistance who gathered the information, as well as those in London who were its compilers and editors, probably lacked a clear understanding of the unit and its history. The name *Garden* was short-lived and *Førerens Garde* was in use at least as early as 17 February 1942. It was the term most widely used in the period up until mid-May 1942 when the final variation – *Førergarden* (which also means the Leader's Guard) – was introduced at Quisling's personal request. Rubber stamps with the variation *Rikshirden Førerens Garde* (the National Hird's Leader's Guard) were being used on documents in March 1942 and there were even cases of Førerens Garde being used after mid-May 1942. For example, a cuffband with those two words in block lettering was being worn on the first pattern dark blue, gala uniform as late as 21 June 1942. As seen in the 7 February 1942 article in *Hirdmannen*, on 5 February, the very day of his appointment (and just four days after Quisling had become Minister President), Gulbrandsen was charged with security at the first meeting of the new State Council at Oslo Palace. He posted what were described as "robust Hird men" armed with police batons on either side of the Palace entrance, while others formed a cordon up the stairs leading to the meeting room on the second floor and elsewhere in and around the building[16]. The guard was divided into two sections (vaktlagene), who were on duty 24 hours a day, standing guard for two-hour shifts, and

Oslo Palace guard house (*vakstuen*), February 1942: Two members of the guard rest between tours of duty: *Hirdmannen*, No. 6, 14 February 1942

RIKSHIRDEN

Hirdskolen i Valdres.

Hirdskolen i Valdres.

Fra 1. mars igangsettes en rekke 1 md.s kurser under ledelse av nestsveitfører TALLERAAS

Eidsiva Hirdskole avsluttet efter å ha utdannet 60 mann.

I begynnelsen av februar sluttet Eidsiva Hirdregiments skole ved Leira i Valdres etter å ha utdannet omlag 60 mann.

Elevene hadde da fått undervisning i praktiske, teoretiske og ideologiske fag samt eksersis og idrett. Skolesjef var nestsveitfører Tallerås, som også skal være skolesjef for de nye kurser som nå settes igang.

Av de øvrige lærere ved Eidsiva Hirdskole skal nevnes intendant Bjørnstad, troppfører Nielsen som underviste i praktiske fag og eksersis, gymnastikklæreren troppfører Fauske og troppfører Scharff, som underviste i musikk. Skolesjefen Tallerås underviste selv i ideologi og ski-eksersis. En fremragende skiløper fra Valdres som vi ikke har fått tak i navnet på, gav Hirdskolens elever instruksjon i skiteknikk.

Hirdmannen's medarbeider har snakket med et par av hirdmennene efter hjemkomsten fra Eidsiva Hirdskole, og det later til at karene er meget vel fornøiet med oppholdet, og mener at de har hatt godt utbytte av det.

I løpet av mars måned åpner skolen atter sine porter for nye kontingenter hirdmenn, idet der settes igang en rekke nye kurser for utdannelse av hirdmenn i de samme fag som [illegible]. Hvert kurs skal strekke seg over omlag en måned. Sjef for skolen blir som ovenfor nevnt nestsveitfører Tallerås.

Hirdmenn som ønsker å delta i kursene kan sende søknad til Rikshirdstabens Utdannelsesavdeling, Tollbugata 10, Oslo.

Ski-instruksjon ved Hirdskolen i Valdres.

Article in *Hirdmannen*, No. 8, 28 February 1942 about the *Hird* School in Valdres

resting during the intervening four hours in the old guard house to the right of the Palace (as one faces its front from Oslo's city centre). The guard house still stands there today, albeit having been renovated and up-dated. The sections formally changed guard at 2 o'clock each afternoon[17]. The original guards and their *lagfører* all came from the Hird. Although it is not clear from which precise units they came, it would be logical to assume that some if not the majority came from the original *Hirdvakt*, which had existed before 1 February 1942. Others could possibly have come from another new *Hird* unit that had been formed in the previous month of January 1942, the so-called "Armed Hird Battalion" (*bevæpende hirdbataljon*), which was expanded in June 1942 into a number of Hird Guard Battalions (*Hirdvaktbataljonen*)[18]. Therefore it is possible that the two dozen or so original guards came from a variety of Hird units, most if not all based in Oslo, and that there were cases of interchange with the existing *Hirdvakt* and the Armed *Hird* Battalion. The large number of *Hird* members that had gathered in Oslo from all over Norway for Quisling's inauguration presented an opportunity to encourage them to volunteer for the new guard. They were addressed at what were described as two large meetings, but the response was disappointing. Emergency action had to be taken to prevent Thronsen's initiative from failure because the new guard unit lacked sufficient men to carry out its duties and expand. It was decided that all of the sixty[19] or so graduates from the Eidsivating *Hird* School (*Hirdskole*) would be transfered to Oslo to bring the unit up to the required strength[20]. This Hird School was located some 88 miles (140 km) north-northwest of Oslo in the small village of Leira i Valdres in the Nord-Aurdal municipality of the Oppland County. It was also known as the Eidsiva *Hird* Regiment's School (Hirdregiments skole) and was commanded by nestsveitfører Tallerås[21], who also taught the students ideology and skiing. On his staff were the intendant, or administrative officer[22], Bjørnstad, *troppfører* Nielsen who taught practical subjects and organized exercises, the music teacher *troppfører* Scharff and the physical training instructor, Torbjørn Fauske. Of these, only Fauske is confirmed to have joined the permanent staff of what was to become *Førergarden*[23]. He claimed that he had joined at the very beginning and he was still the *Førergarden* sports leader (*idrettsleder*) in January 1944, by which time he had been promoted to the rank of *løytnant*[24]. The sixty or so young men transferred to Oslo with Fauske had graduated in early February 1942 after receiving instruction in practical, theoretical and ideological subjects, as well as having taken part in exercises and sport. When interrogated after the war, Gulbrandsen stated that the men who had come from the Leira school had undertaken to serve there for a pre-determined period of time.

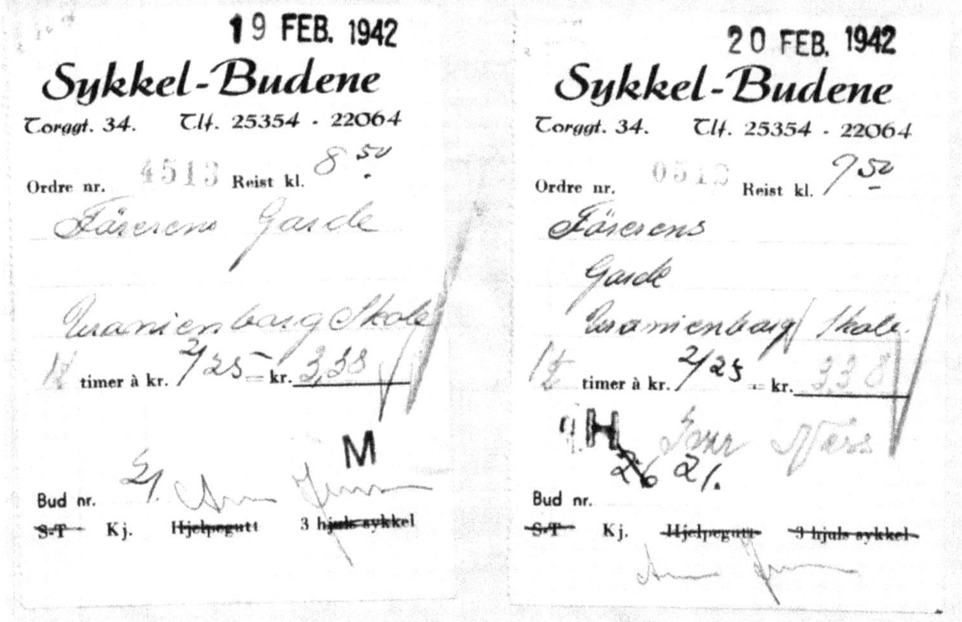

19 FEB. 1942

Sykkel-Budene

Torggt. 34. Tlf. 25354 - 22064

Ordre nr. 4513 Reist kl. 8 50

Førerens Garde

Uranienborg Skole

1½ timer à kr. 2.25 = kr. 3.38

M

Bud nr. 21.

~~S-T~~ Kj. ~~Hjelpegutt~~ 3 ~~hjuls sykkel~~

20 FEB. 1942

Sykkel-Budene

Torggt. 34. Tlf. 25354 - 22064

Ordre nr. Reist kl. 7 50

Førerens Garde

Uranienborg Skole

1½ timer à kr. 2.25 = kr. 3.38

H

Bud nr. 21.

~~S-T~~ Kj. ~~Hjelpegutt~~ ~~3 hjuls sykkel~~

Receipts for bicycle courier services dated 19 & 20 February 1942 and made out to *"Førerens Garde"* at the Uranienborg School. *Riksarkiv* reference PA-766

However, when this period ended and they were still serving in Quisling's guard, they were encouraged to stay on, and some who were with the guard for more than two months undertook to remain for six. After the graduates' departure from Leira, the school

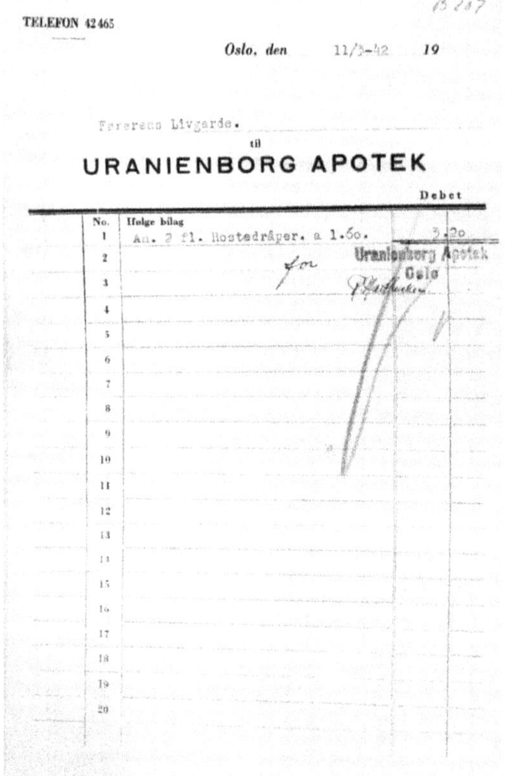

B 187

TELEFON 42465

Oslo, den 11/3-42 19

Førerens Livgarde.

til

URANIENBORG APOTEK

No.	Ifølge bilag	Debet
1	An. 2 fl. Hostedråper. a 1.5o.	3.2o
2		
3		
4		
5		
6		
7		
8		
9		
10		
11		
12		
13		
14		
15		
16		
17		
18		
19		
20		

for Uranienborg Apotek Oslo

Receipt for cough drops issued to "*Førerens Livgarde*" by the Uranienborg pharmacy on 11 March 1942. *Riksarkiv* reference PA-766

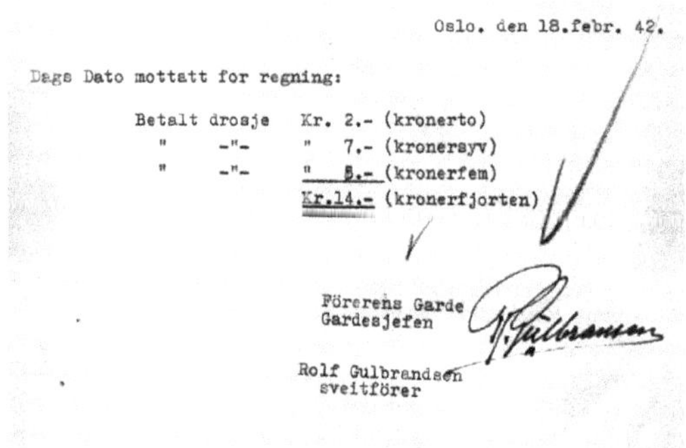

Oslo. den 18.febr. 42.

Dags Dato mottatt for regning:

Betalt drosje Kr. 2.- (kronerto)
" -"- " 7.- (kronersyv)
" -"- " 5.- (kronerfem)
Kr.14.- (kronerfjorten)

Förerens Garde
Gardesjefen

Rolf Gulbrandsen
sveitförer

Gulbrandsen's signed claim for reimbursement of 3 taxi rides in Oslo, 18 February 1942. *Riksarkiv* reference PA-766

resumed its activities and Talleräs began to hold a series of one-month courses on 1 March 1942. So it was that at some time in February 1942, the sixty or so *Hird* graduates were brought to Oslo to reinforce the strength of the new unit and were barracked along with the existing guards at the Uranienborg School, a stone's throw from the Palace. While this made a mockery of the purely voluntary nature of the new guard unit early on in its history, it was seen as a stopgap and emergency measure that would only continue until the required number of Hird members stepped forward to fill the ranks of the new unit from all over Norway. On 20 April 1942, when Gulbrandsen was replaced as the unit's chief and the guard unit was detached from the *Hird*, most of the Leira cadets were still there amongst the one hundred or so young men who constituted the guard at that point. The immediate need for men having been satisfied, Gulbrandsen then sent out a written invitation to the commanders of the regional *Hird* regiments[25] (these were the same men who had been encouraged — if not instructed — to send representatives to Oslo for the make-believe rally that in fact turned out to be Quisling's inauguration). He invited them to provide volunteers for a six-month tour of duty in what, at that stage, had not yet been given a formal name and was still being referred to generically as a *Hird* special unit (*spesialavdeling*). According to Gulbrandsen, no formal undertaking was required and the volunteers did not have to take an oath[26]. The numerous purchase invoices in the state archives in Oslo provide an idea of how preparations were being made and supplies provided to the new unit in the second half of February 1942, which was by then being

Oslo, den 17. februar.1942.

Efter ordre fra Gardesjefen for Förerens Garde
1 -ett- trikkekort Kr. 2.10.

Mottatt:
Gunnar Andresen
Gunnar Andresen
Kvartermester

Receipt for a tram card ordered by the commander of what was called *Førerens Garde*, signed by *kvartermester* Gunnar Andresen and dated 17 February 1942. *Riksarkiv* reference PA-766

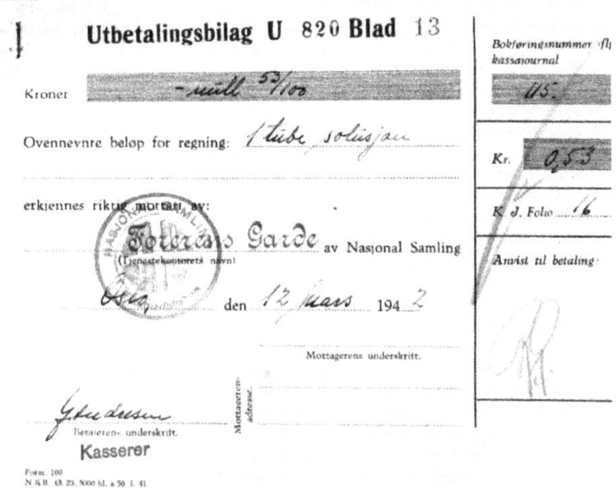

1 Utbetalingsbilag U 820 Blad 13

Kroner -null- 53/100

Ovennevnte beløp for regning: 1 tube solisjan

erkjennes riktig mottatt av:

Förerens Garde av Nasjonal Samling
(Tjenestekontorets navn)

Oslo den 12 mars 1942

Mottagerens underskrift.

Betalerens underskrift.
Kasserer

Bokføringsnummer i kassajournal: 115

Kr. 0,53

K. J. Folio 16

Anvist til betaling

The red in-line ink stamp *"Førerens Garde"* in the space reserved for the N.S. "service office" on a payment voucher dated 12 March 1942 and signed by the unit's cashier. *Riksarkiv* reference PA-766

referred to as *"Førerens Garde"*: the shopping list was varied and included cooking and office equipment, books, book binding, bread, bicycle couriers, tram tickets and medication(27) that were purchased between 18 and 26 February. Specific supplies were purchased via the *Hird* Headquarters, such as 14 pairs of boots on 20 February 1942. Two invoices, dated 19 and 20 February, were addressed to the Uranienborg School. On 18 February, guard chief (*Gardesjefen*) of *Förerens Garde*, *sveitförer* Rolf Gulbrandsen, also claimed reimbursement for three taxi rides which, if one also considers the tram tickets, suggests that at that stage at least the unit lacked any means of transport of its own. While at the Uranienborg School, the *Hird* graduates continued to be subject to *Hird* rules and regulations while on and off duty, and wore their *Hird* uniforms. In addition to their guard duties, they underwent military training and took part in gymnastics and sport(28). Recruitment began in earnest in mid-March 1942 when the unit numbered 90 men. The German Security Police in Oslo described it as the start of an *"intense newspaper campaign"*, which was launched to attract volunteers for the new unit, especially from the *Hird*(29). The following appeal to members of the *Hird* to join was published on the front page of *Hirdmannen*, No. 10, 14 March 1942:

THE LEADER'S GUARD (FØRERENS GARDE).

Men of the Hird! It is a time of expansion in our country today. The new Norway, a national socialist Norway, takes shape. The Norwegians have once again received a Norwegian-born Leader who, with a sure hand, takes his people towards the goal: a free and happy Norway. Our tasks are getting greater, we have to work and work again. The *Hird* must go forward in the fight at the Leader's side, that is our place! If we cannot hold our position as the most sacrificial and energetic members of the Nasjonal Samling, then we are unworthy of being Hird men. These days, the National *Hird* has received a new special unit: the Leader's Guard. Again, *Hird* men stand guard over their Leader, as was the custom in Norway's period of greatness. The Leader's Guard is a guard and parade unit that is barracked in Oslo. The men of the Guard will still be where the master is and units of the Guard provide security and representation on important occasions. It is a glorious task, and only the best *Hird* men will have the opportunity to join. By the way, the conditions for the participants are that they be

at least 1.72 m (5′ 8″) in height
and between 18 and 26 years of age.

The Leader's Guard will receive particularly good training and first-class equipment. The service period is 3-4 months. Participants receive full board and free uniform as well as kr. 1.50 per day.

FØRERENS GARDE

Blå uniform. Enkelt- knappet jakke med belte. Hvite beiser i benklærne. Brun skjorte med sort slips. Båtlue.

Menig gardist

195

Despite going to press in early 1943, the unit is still described as *"Førerens Garde"* on page 195 of NS Årbok 1942 when illustrating and describing the gala uniform, when in fact that name had been changed to *"Førergarden"* at Quisling's request in mid-May 1942

The new unit was not to stay at the Uranienborg School for long. In April the German armed forces (*Wehrmacht*) decided it needed to use the building and gave Carlson what has been described as "embarrassingly short notice" that his men had to vacate the school and move elsewhere[30]. During April or presumably soon after being evicted they were transferred with the original *Hird* members of the unit to new quarters in Bygdøy, not far from Quisling's official residence, Gimle, the former Villa Grande[31]. The German Security Police reported on 31 March 1942 that the age limit, which was to be between 18 and 26, had not been respected in the case of *Hird* members taken into the unit by that date(32). The initial age limit of 26 would later be increased to 30, but this was compensated in part by them having to be slightly taller (175 cm or 5′ 9″)(33). Moreoever, posters printed in August 1943 would state that Quisling expected all male members of the N.S. (not just the *Hird*) between the ages of 17 and 35 to join what had by then become known as Førergarden.

Notes

(1) As stated in point 1. of an undated report by the Education Department of the *Hird* Headquarters (*Rikshirden, Hirdstaben Utd. Avd., Førergarde*).

(2) The only source found so far for this "Leader's Guard" is Luihn: *De illegale avisene. Den frie, hemmelige pressen i Norge under okkupasjonen*, page 86, quoted by Hoidal, *Quisling: A Study in Treason*, page 550, where he writes "*élite members of his street fighters, known as the Førerhird, were installed as guards at the palace, occupying the posts previously patrolled by the Royal Guard*". It is possible that this was in fact an inaccurate reference to the *Hird* Guard (*Hirdvakten*).

(3) Tollbugt. (short for Tollbugata) is shown in the N.S. Årbok 1944, page 68; however, it is Tollbodgaten in *Nasjonal Samling Telefonliste og Adressebok, January 1945*, page 7. The difference in spelling was the result of the modernization of the Norwegian language and today the street is named Tollbugata.

(4) The three levels of protection are given by Quisling's authorative biographer, Dahl, *Quisling: A Study in Treachery*, pages 332/334, but he was mistaken insofar as Quisling's adjutants were concerned. As explained to the author by the late Bjørn Jervås in his e-mail of 15 December 2008, Quisling's adjutants were not part of his security and in fact were not even armed. Quisling's private adjutant/secretary was Per Jahr, who at first wore his Young *Hird* (*Unghird*) uniform. For some reason, in 1944, he was given the rank of *overløytnant* (despite having had no military training) and ordered to wear *Førergarden* uniform (even though he was not then a member of that unit). Jahr eventually became a member of *Førergarden* on 18 March 1944) After Jahr in rank came *kaptein* Carl Haakon Langlie, Chief of the Adjutant's Staff (*Sjef for Adjutantsstaben*), a position which was also established on 1 February 1942. The adjutants themselves were selected from the *Rikshird*, Germanske SS Norge, Police and A.T. From 1943 onwards each of them should have held at least the rank of kaptein and served as Quisling's adjutant for 3 months. Langlie was 1st Adjutant and Head of the Adjutant's Staff (*1ste adjutant og sjef for adjutantsstaben*) in 1942 (shown in the NS Årbok 1942, page 149, as Chief-of-Staff — *Stabsjef*) and 1943. In 1942 three adjutants are known, løytnant Bertel Brun, Sverre Wille (a former *fenrik* in the Navy) and former Air Force *løytnant* Per Carlson, who would later command *Førergarden* for over 23 of its 39-month life: from 20 April 1942 to 1 April 1944 (*Norges Statskalender 1942*, page 3/4). No names were given for 1943 (*Norges Statskalender 1942*, pages 3/4). Norwegian military intelligence in London gave Langlie and Sven Åge Frisch as Quisling's two adjutants in a report up-dated to 1 December 1944 (Norwegian Nazi Organizations, I.F.O. II 696/45, High Command, Royal Norwegian Forces, 2nd Department, London, 15 February 1945, page 8). Liste Nr. 1 gives Bjarne Vold and Nils Wangen as two of Quisling's other adjutants. Those who were in practice closest to Quisling and would have protected him from attack first formed a small group of policemen named the "Civil Guard" (*Sivilvakten*), who had their own room at Oslo Palace. In late 1944 or early 1945 when the time had come for him to really need protection, a group of fifteen or so men made up of ultra-loyal former *Waffen-SS* front fighters named "*the Guests*" were at Gimle under *SS-Untersturmführer der Reserve* Bjørn Østring, himself an *overløytnant* in *Førergarden*.

(5) Hewins was clearly confused in his book *Quisling: Prophet without Honour*, page 319, when he wrote that "*the guard of honor for the new Minister-President*" at the ceremony held on 1 February 1942 "*was formed by detachments of seven famous Norwegian Army regiments, whose presence underlined the new start to be made with Defense*". Hewins may not have appreciated that a new unit was born that day from the *Hird*, and that this Guard would be drawn from the territorial regiments of the *Hird* (which most authors have stated were seven, but in fact they were numbered up to 9); after all, at that time there was no Norwegian army.

(6) At least eight can be seen standing along one side wall in the official newsreel and photographs of the ceremony, suggesting there were at least twice that number within the Knights' Hall itself.

(7) Born on 1 February 1917, sharing his birthday with Quisling's appointment as Minister President and the official establishment of Førergarden, Thronsen had joined the N.S. in 1933. Effective 15 November 1940 he was appointed as acting Chief of Staff of the *Hird*, while remaining the *Hird* leader for Greater Oslo, a position he

held until 5 February 1941 (*Hird* Orders of 14 November 1940 and 25 January 1941, published in *Hirdmannen* Nos. 1, 16 November 1940 and 7, 1 February 1941, respectively). On that date he held the *Hird* rank of nestregimentfører and took leave of absence to serve in *SS Regiment "Nordland"* on the Eastern Front, returning to resume that same post again on 7 January 1942 (his resumption of the post was reported in *Hirdmannen*, No. 1, 10 January 1942). Quisling held him in high regard and he was among the select group of N.S. leaders who would accompany the newly appointed Minister President to visit Hitler in Berlin on 13 February 1942. Thorvald's brother, John, was the N.S. Economics Chief (*riksøkonomisjef*) who was disgraced in 1943 when accused of corruption (see *Norsk Krigsleksikon*, pages 420 and 421). While Thorvald is reported to have been involved in the scandal, reports that this resulted in his being pressurized into leaving the *Hird* in February 1944 would appear unfounded, as Thronsen commanded the 1st Hird Command (*1. Hirdfordeling*) from 1 February to at least November 1944 and was promoted from nestregimentfører to regimentfører with effect from 1 September 1944. After the liberation, he was excused from prosecution on the grounds of insanity and died on 15 June 2003. His brother John was sentenced to 8 years forced labor, but was released in 1949.

(8) That the initiative to form what would become *Førergarden* came from Thronsen is confi rmed in point 1 of the aforementioned undated report by the Education Department of the Hird Headquarters and in *Hirdmannen*, No. 5, 29 January 1944. It is possible that he felt responsible for this decision given that the existing guard unit was a part of the *Hird*.

(9) See Chapter 10 for a biographical summary.

(10) *Hirdmannen*, 7 February 1942.

(11) *Die Ehrenwache am Osloer Schloss, den Amtssitz des Ministerpräsidenten, einer Abteilung Hird übernommen.*

(12) Whoever created the captions for the book's photographs may have had the Norwegian word "*Avdeling*" in mind, which corresponds to the more generic "department" or "unit".

(13) The guard house (known as vakstuen in 1942, but today Gardevaktstua), was built in 1845 and remains as it was to this day.

(14) Undated report *Førergarden, Rikshirden/Hirdstaben Utd. Avd.* Per Carlson, who replaced Gulbrandsen as chief of the guard unit on 20 April 1942, appears to have been mistaken when he testified at Quisling's postwar trial that the unit's name had been changed from *Vakten* (also meaning "the Guard") on the day he assumed command.

(15) This title was used on a receipt dated 11 March 1942.

(16) *Hirdmannen*, No. 5, 7 February 1942, and Veum, *Nådeløse Nordmenn. Hirden 1933-1945*, pages 112/114. Subsequent coverage of Førergarden published in February 1944 gave the false impression that it had actually been formed on 1 February 1942, the very same day Quisling became Minister President, when in fact that was only the day that *Hird* men began to guard Oslo Palace and a guard unit as such was not formed until some days later (Munin, No. 4, 2nd February 1944 issue, page 3). According to Dahl, op.cit., page 334, the *Hird* had taken on the task of guarding the palace in February 1942 (he does not give a precise date), armed with police truncheons, and *Førergarden* was formed into a separate entity in April 1942, financed directly out of the state budget from 1943. As early as 20 February 1942 an order was placed with the Hird H.Q. warehouse for 12 pairs of boots (Rekr. N. 2907).

(17) Veum, op.cit., page 114.

(18) Veum, op.cit., pages 387 and 388. 9 e *Hird* Guard Battalions were subsequently renamed a number of times: in September 1942 to the "Guard Battalion Norway" (*Vaktbataljon Norge*) suggesting a reduction in strength; in November 1942 to SS Guard Battalion Norway (*SS-Vaktbataljon Norge*); and finally in January 1943 to *SS-Vaktbataljon*. The majority of men in the *Hird* Guard Battalions were recruited from the *Hird*. Originally these battalions guarded factories and industrial plants as well as foreign prisoners of war, and they gained a reputation for brutal treatment of Yugoslav POWs in northern Norway (see Veum, op.cit., page 371, who lists the names and provides biographical details of 352 members of *Hird* Guard Battalions between pages 567 and 673.)

(19) Sources vary as to the exact number of *Hird* graduates who were transferred from the Leira school, ranging from as many as 70 (report by Detective Inspector Johannes Gartå dated 13 February 1946 on his interrogation the previous day of Rolf Gulbrandsen) to as little as 30 or 40 (Veum, op.cit., page 114), whereas both "60" and "about 60" are given in the article on the school in Hirdmannen, No. 8, 28 February 1942.

[20] *Hirdmannen*, No. 5, 29 January 1944. It is to be noted that the article makes no mention of the graduates going to Oslo to reinforce the strength of Quisling's new bodyguard unit, presumably as the difficulties encountered in forming it were not to be made public, if not actually kept secret.

[21] It is possible that the person listed as Paul Tallerås in the not always accurate and reliable Liste Nr. 1 (entry 27 on page 726) was in fact the commander of the *Hird* school in Leira, Oppland, given that he was shown as coming from Hadeland and to have been an instructor at a *Hird* leaders' course in Gjövik, as both Hadeland (a district) and Gjövik (a town and municipality) are located in the Oppland county. The entry also gave his rank as not only in the N.S. (*NS-sveitfører*) but also in the *Hird* (*Troppsfører i Hirden*) and that he was head of a Boy's *Hird* Section Leaders' School (*Skolesjef ved guttehirdens lagførerskole*).

[22] The English equivalent of the German (and presumably Norwegian) military term Intendant is given as "intendant, administrative offi cer" in German Military Abbreviations, Special Series, No. 12, MIS 461, Military Intelligence Service, War Department, Washington, DC, 12 April 1943, page 89. In the British Army it would be translated as "quartermaster" or "G4 supply offi cer" (Simon Orchard, e-mail to the author, 20 July 2020), but "quartermaster" has not been used here to avoid confusion with the NCO administrative rank in *Førergarden* of "*kvartermester*", abbreviated "*kvm.*", which was equivalent to "*kommandersjant*", abbreviated "*ks.*". The German word Intendant was defined in 1942 as an "official (*Wehrmachtbeamter*) on formation staff in charge of administration of supplies, transport, financial matters, etc." (Vocabulary of German Military Terms and Abbreviations, revised to 1942, General Staff , the War Office, His Majesty's Stationery Office, London, April 1943, page 69). A German military dictionary published in 1943 (Eitzen Deutsche — Englisches Englisch — Deutsches Militär-Wörterbuch, 3. Auflage, Verlag "*Offene Worte*", Berlin, 1943) gave "commissariat officer" for Intendant. The judgement in the post-war treason trial of Olaf Woxen Johansen, who as will be seen was Førergarden's intendant from 1 June 1942 until 8 May 1945, stated that "*he was in charge of everything that had to do with Førergarden's catering, equipment, management of funds, salaries, etc. (alt som hadde med førergardens forpleining, utstyr, forvaltning av pengemidler, lønninger m.v. å gjøre)*". Intendant was also used to describe a highranking official or administrator in France, Spain and Portugal and in territories in South America.

[23] It is possible that the school's Nielsen was nestsveitfører Paul Nielsen, born in Moss on 29 May 1910, who served with Førergarden until December 1942.

[24] *Hirdmannen*, No. 5, 29 January 1944.

[25] According to most published studies of the *Hird*, such as the works of Veum and Littlejohn, there were seven *Hird* regiments, when in fact two more have been found in research for this book, which were either additional or the result of re-numbering.

[26] Report by Detective Inspector Johannes Gartå dated 13 February 1946 on his interrogation the previous day of Rolf Gulbrandsen. This is in contradiction to Veum who writes that one of the deterrents to volunteering for service in Quisling's guard was the requirement that one had to sign a declaration of loyalty to the unit's chief (op.cit., page 115 and footnote 369, quoting Riksadvokatens meddelelsesblad [Public Prosecutions Notification Sheet] of December 1946, number 24, page 15). While there is no reference to any oath on either side of either of the two versions of the FGU IV index cards, spaces for entries for the date and place the *Hird* oath (*Hirdeden*) and the *Førergarden* oath of loyaltry (*Troskapsed i Førergarden*) were taken are provided on pages 7 and 9 respectively of the respective organizations' Service Books and on the back of the Førergarden Reserve card for the date and place the oath of allegiance to the Leader (Førered) was taken. Gartå's report is the source of the following facts: Gulbrandsen's meeting with Thronsen; the unit would guard Quisling at the Palace; volunteers would come from *Hird* units gathered in Oslo at the time; there were two large meetings; the *Hird* school from Leira provided some 70 (sic; the number was 60, or thereabouts) young men who were lodged at the Uranienborg School; and mailed requests were sent out to the commanders of the *Hird* regiments (presumably after they had returned to their homes from Oslo).

[27] An invoice from a pharmacist named Uranienborg Apotek dated 19 February 1942 was for unspecified medication required by guards numbered 6 (Nilsen), 7 (Bakken), 28 (Kyllo), 64 (Winnes) and 65 (Gjølberg); another dated 11 March 1942 was for cough drops.

[28] Report by Detective Inspector Johannes Gartå dated 13 February 1946 on his interrogation the previous day of Rolf Gulbrandsen.

[29] BdSudSD Oslo, Meldungen aus Norwegen Nr. 37 vom 31. März 1942, i.V. unterzeichnet Noot, Anlage

"Schwedische Presse, Meldungen über Norwegen" nicht ediert. BA R 70/N/7, Bl. 2-69, Meldungen aus Norwegen 1940 — 1945, Teilband II, page 583.

(30) Lars Borgersrud: op. cit, page 342.

(31) Veum, op.cit., page 124, confirms the transfer, but not the date.

(32) BdSudSD Oslo, Meldungen aus Norwegen Nr. 37 vom 31. März 1942, i.V. unterzeichnet Noot, Anlage *"Schwedische Presse, Meldungen über Norwegen"* nicht ediert. BA R 70/N/7, Bl. 2-69, Meldungen aus Norwegen 1940 — 1945, Teilband II, page 583.

(33) Undated report Førergarden, Rikshirden/Hirdstaben Utd. Avd..

TITOLI PUBBLICATI - ALREADY PUBLISHING

THE AXIS FORCES - NUMBER 1 -JANUARY 2017
WW2 AXIS FORCES

THE AXIS FORCES - NUMBER 2 - APRIL 2017
WW2 AXIS FORCES

THE AXIS FORCES - NUMBER 3 - JULY 2017
WW2 AXIS FORCES

THE AXIS FORCES -NUMBER 4- OCTOBER 2017
WW2 AXIS FORCES

THE AXIS FORCES -NUMBER 5- JANUARY 2018
WW2 AXIS FORCES

THE AXIS FORCES -NUMBER 6- APRIL 2018
WW2 AXIS FORCES

THE AXIS FORCES -NUMBER 7- JULY 2018
WW2 AXIS FORCES

THE AXIS FORCES -NUMBER 8- OCTOBER 2018
PER L'ONORE
X' FLOTTIGLIA MAS
WW2 AXIS FORCES

THE AXIS FORCES 9 - FEBRUARY 2019
WW2 AXIS FORCES

THE AXIS FORCES 10 - MAY 2019
WW2 AXIS FORCES

THE AXIS FORCES 11 - AUGUST 2019
WW2 AXIS FORCES

THE AXIS FORCES 12 - DECEMBER 2019
WW2 AXIS FORCES

WW2 AXIS FORCES

www.ingramcontent.com/pod-product-compliance
Ingram Content Group UK Ltd.
Pitfield, Milton Keynes, MK11 3LW, UK
UKHW061828190726
13853UKWH00009B/2487